ALABAMA

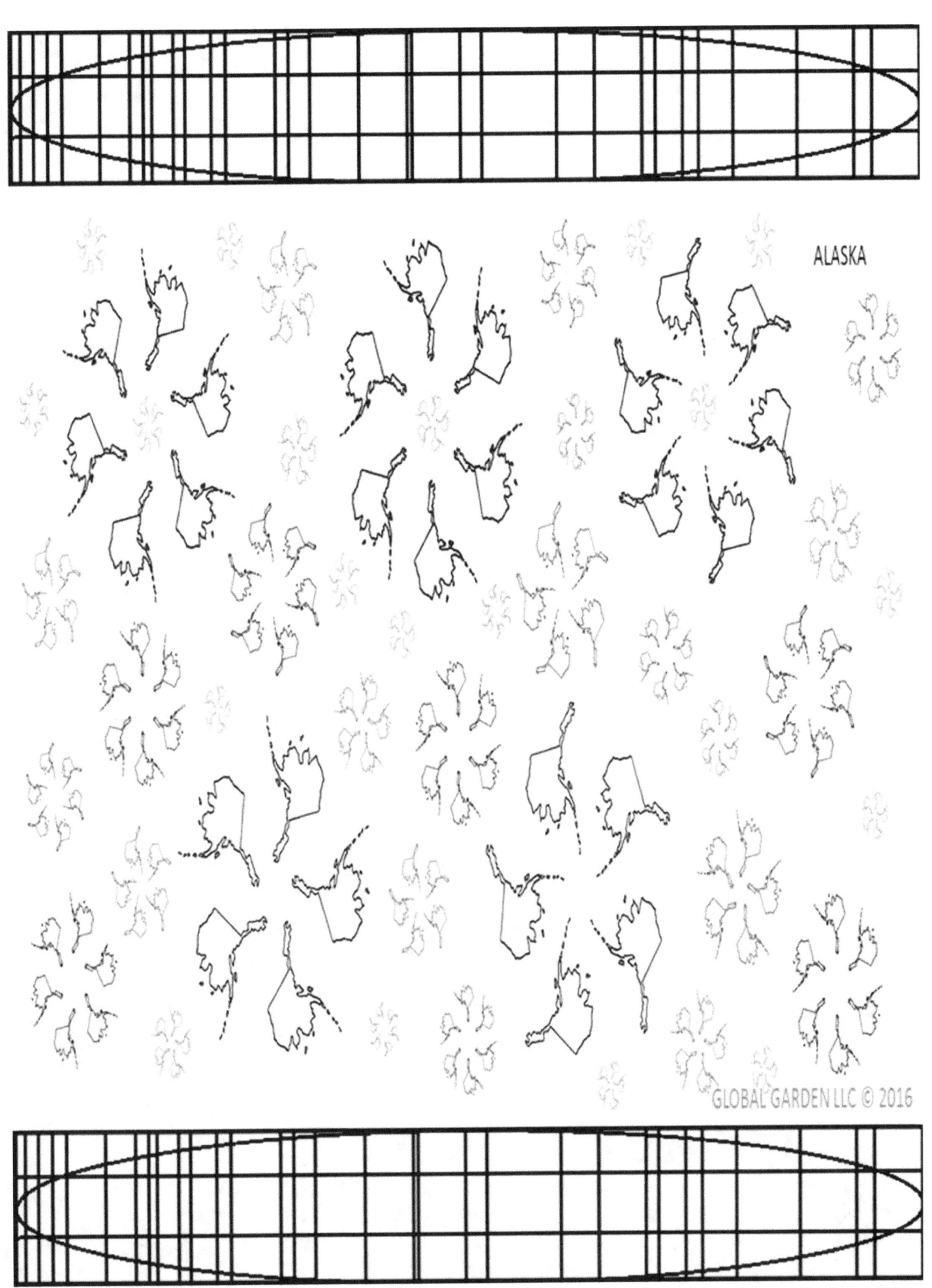

ALASKA

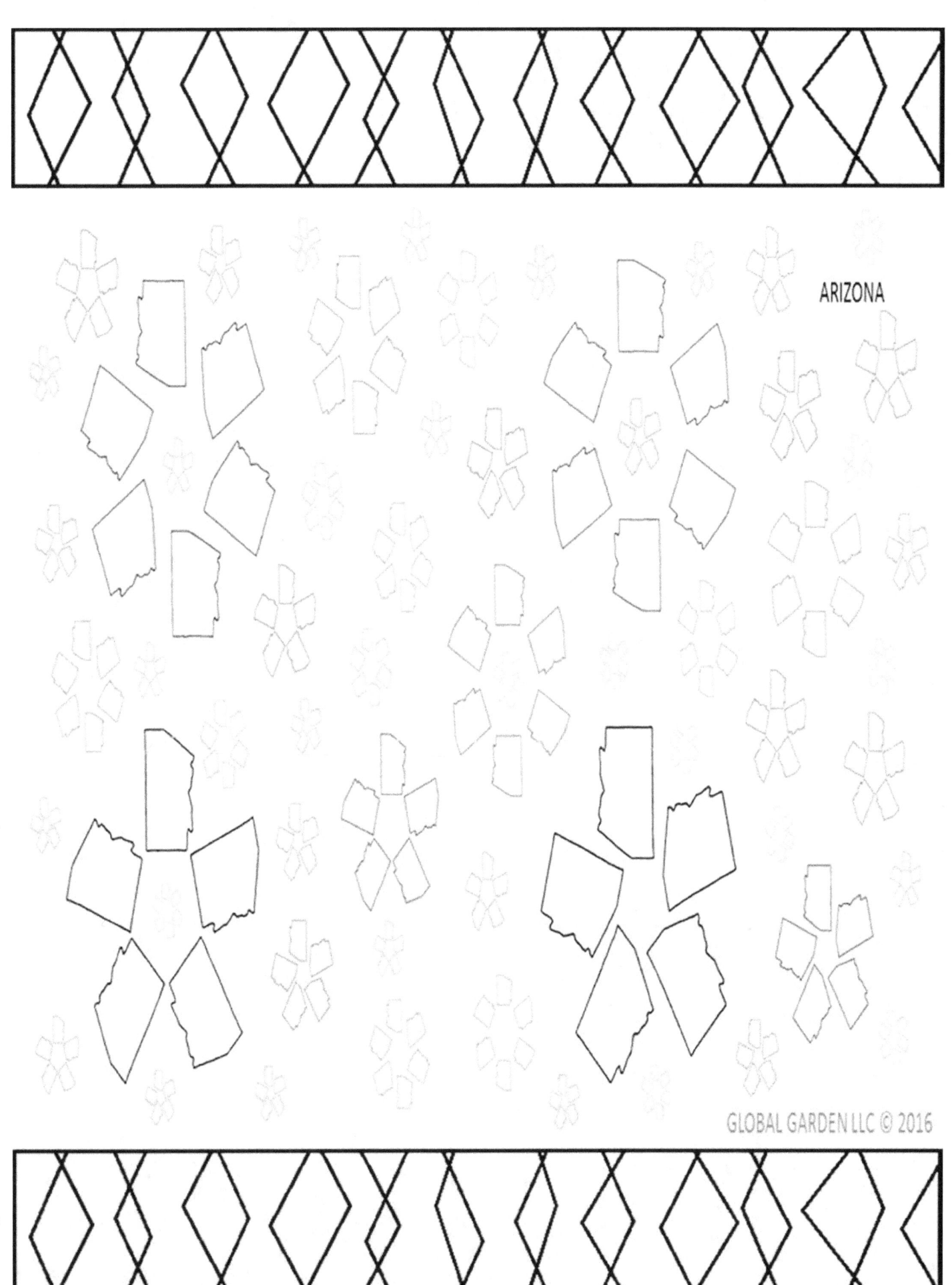

ARIZONA

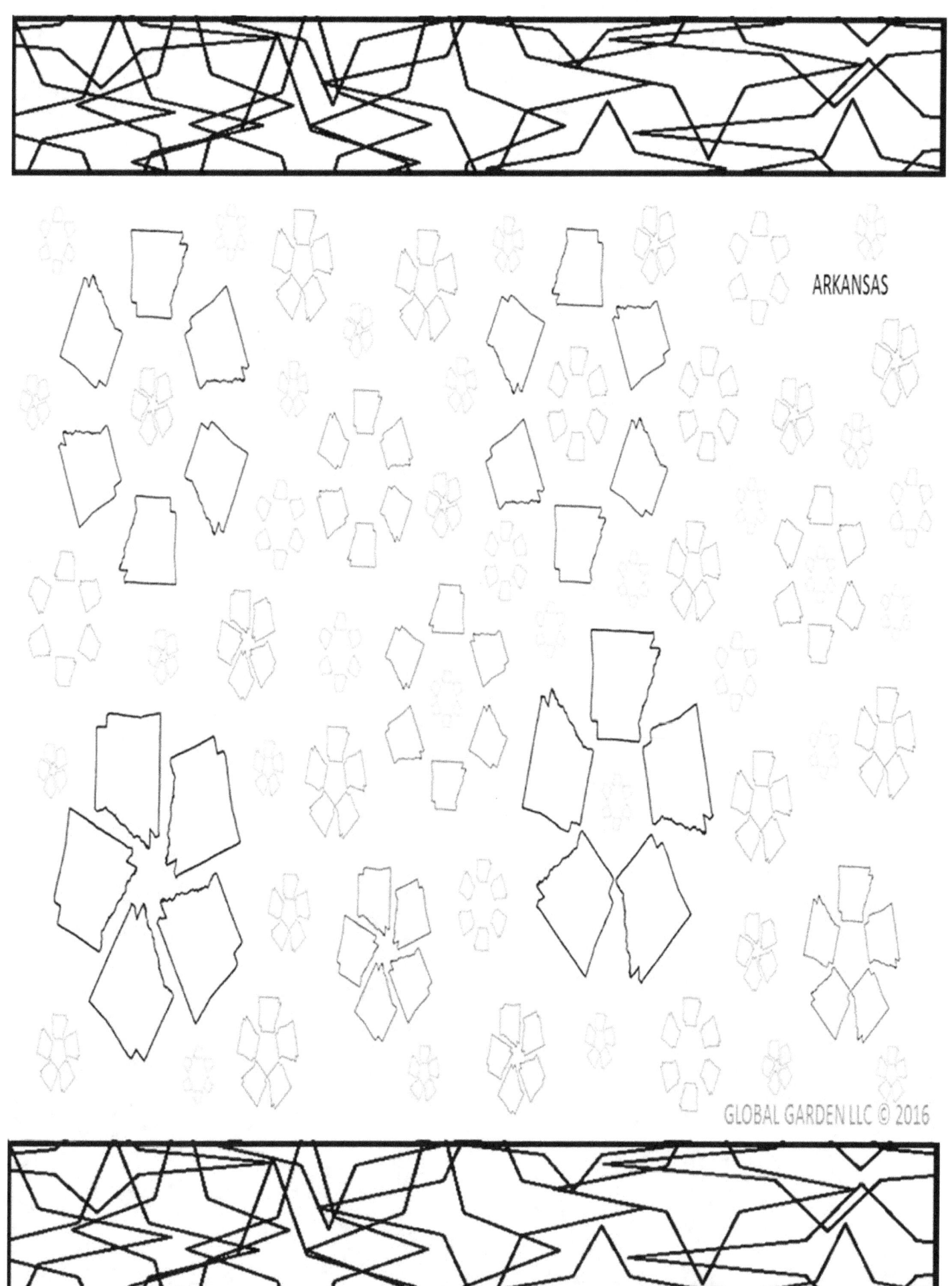

ARKANSAS

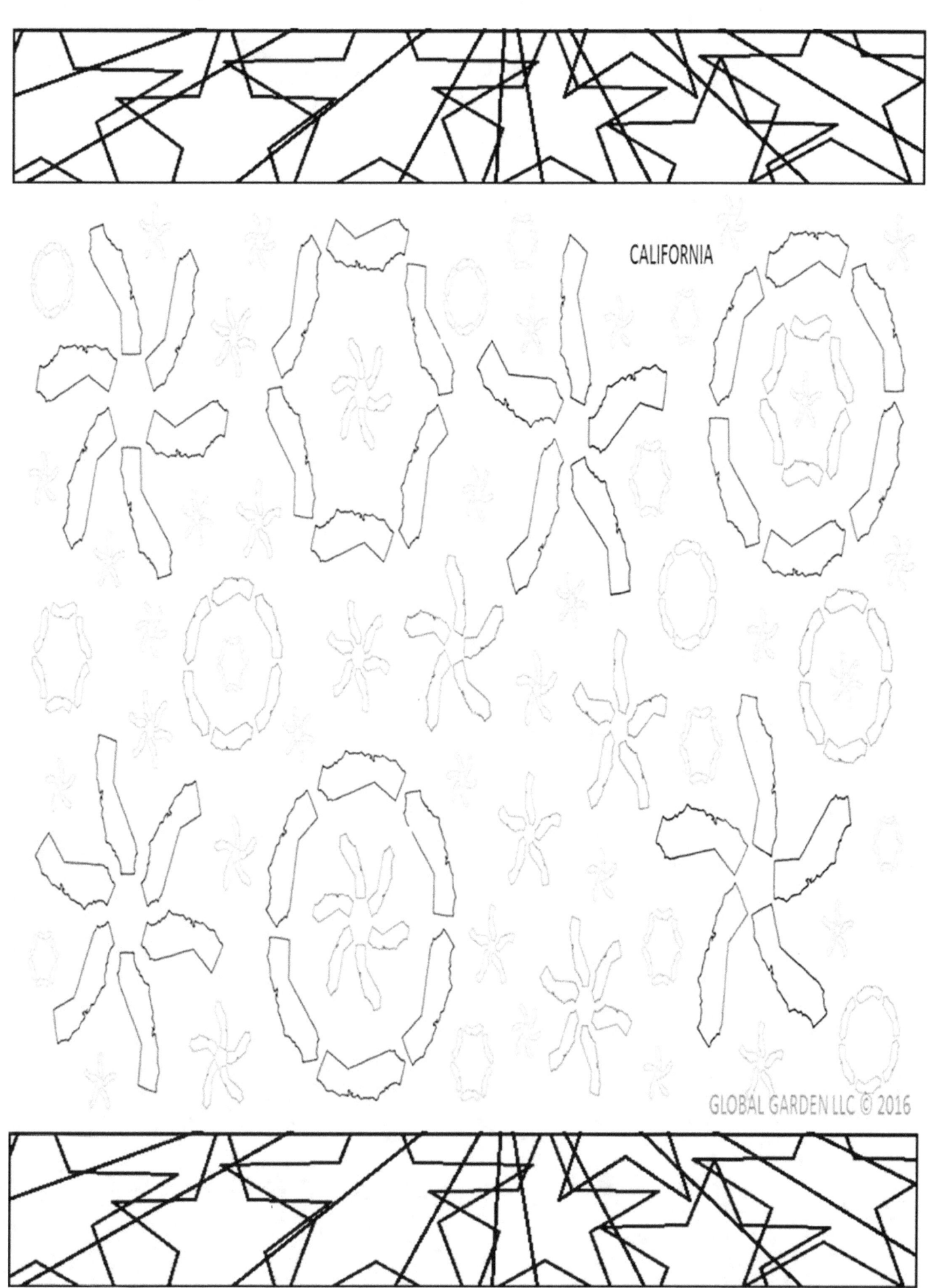

CALIFORNIA

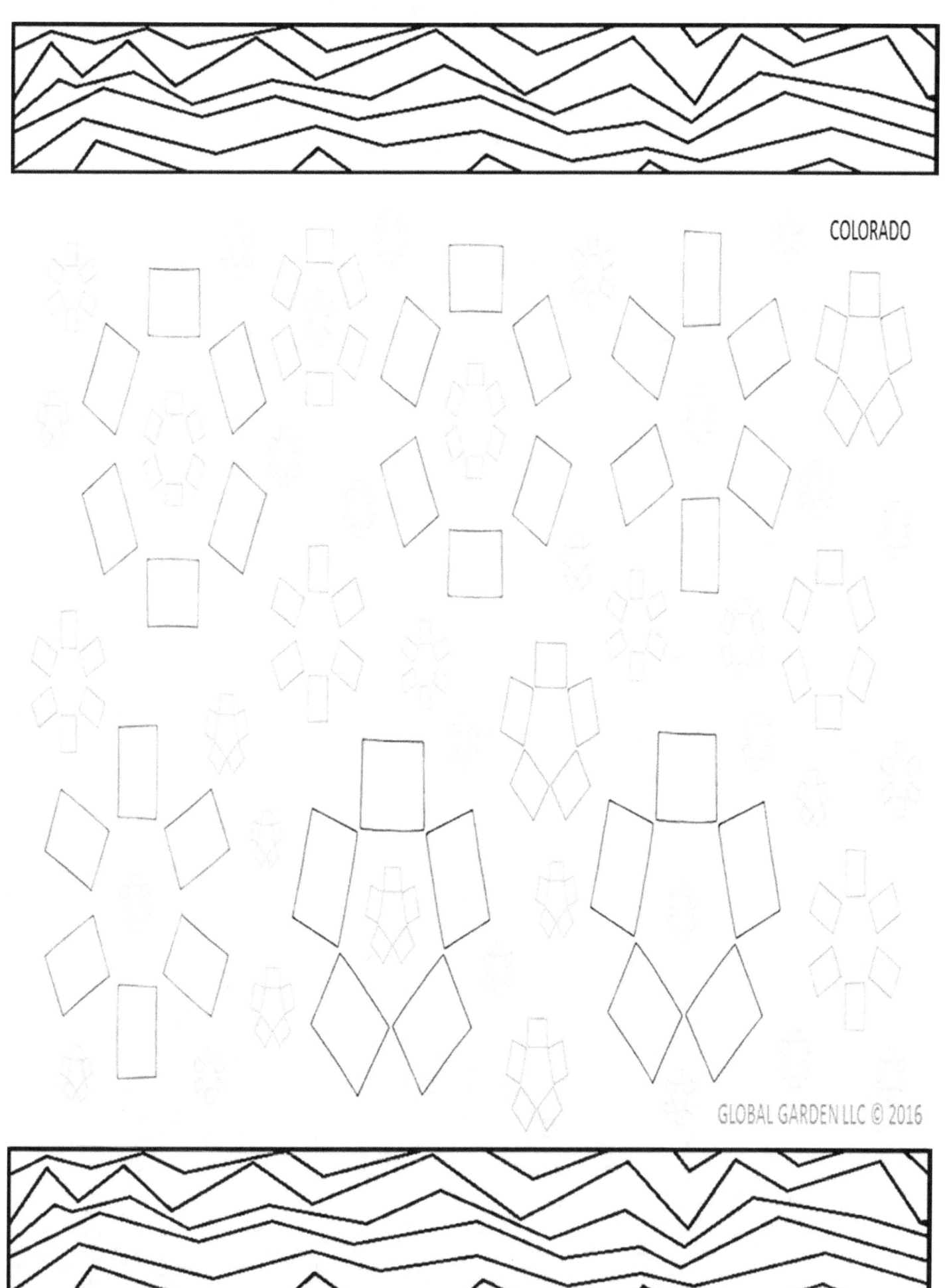

COLORADO

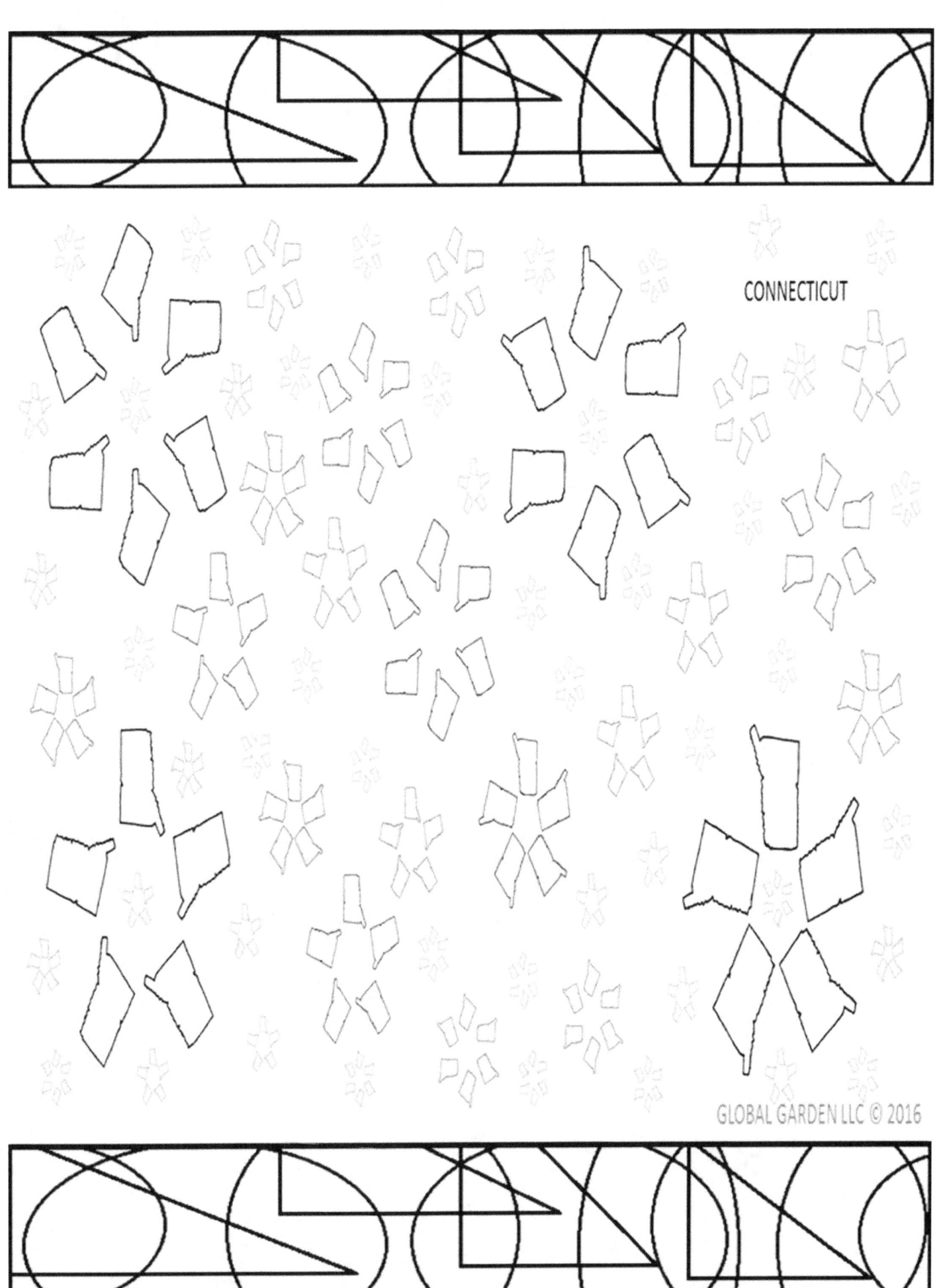

CONNECTICUT

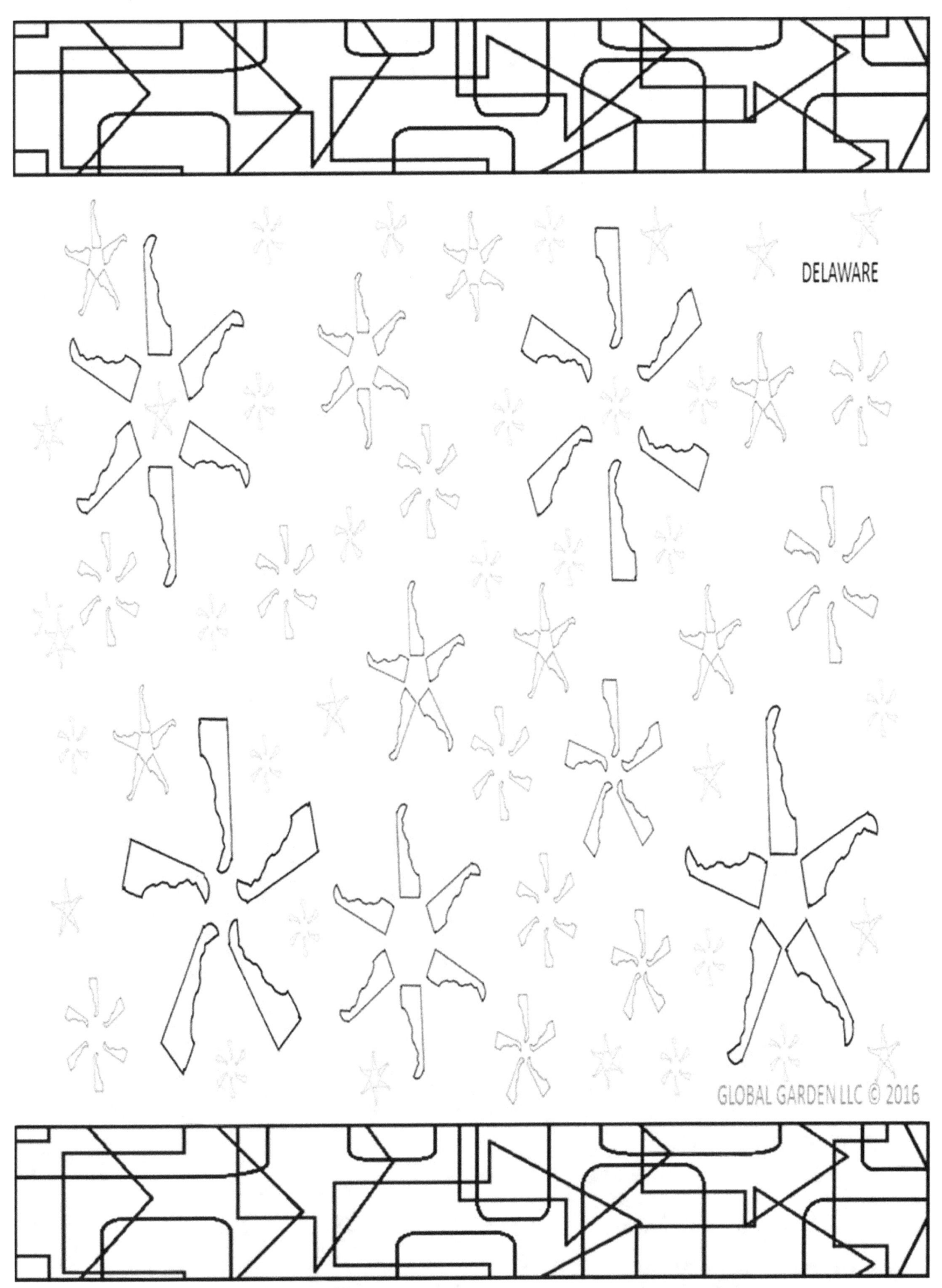

DELAWARE

FLORIDA

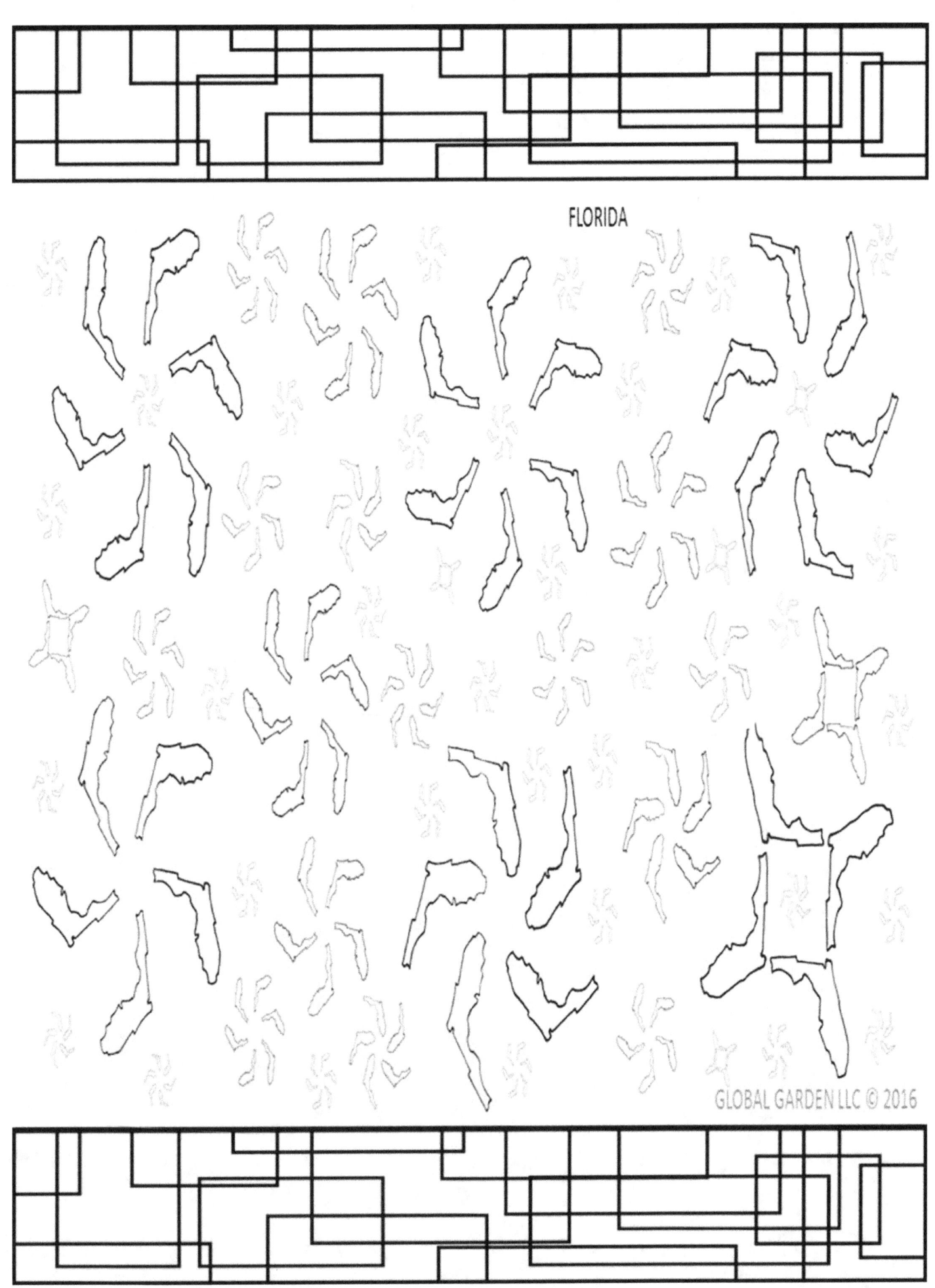

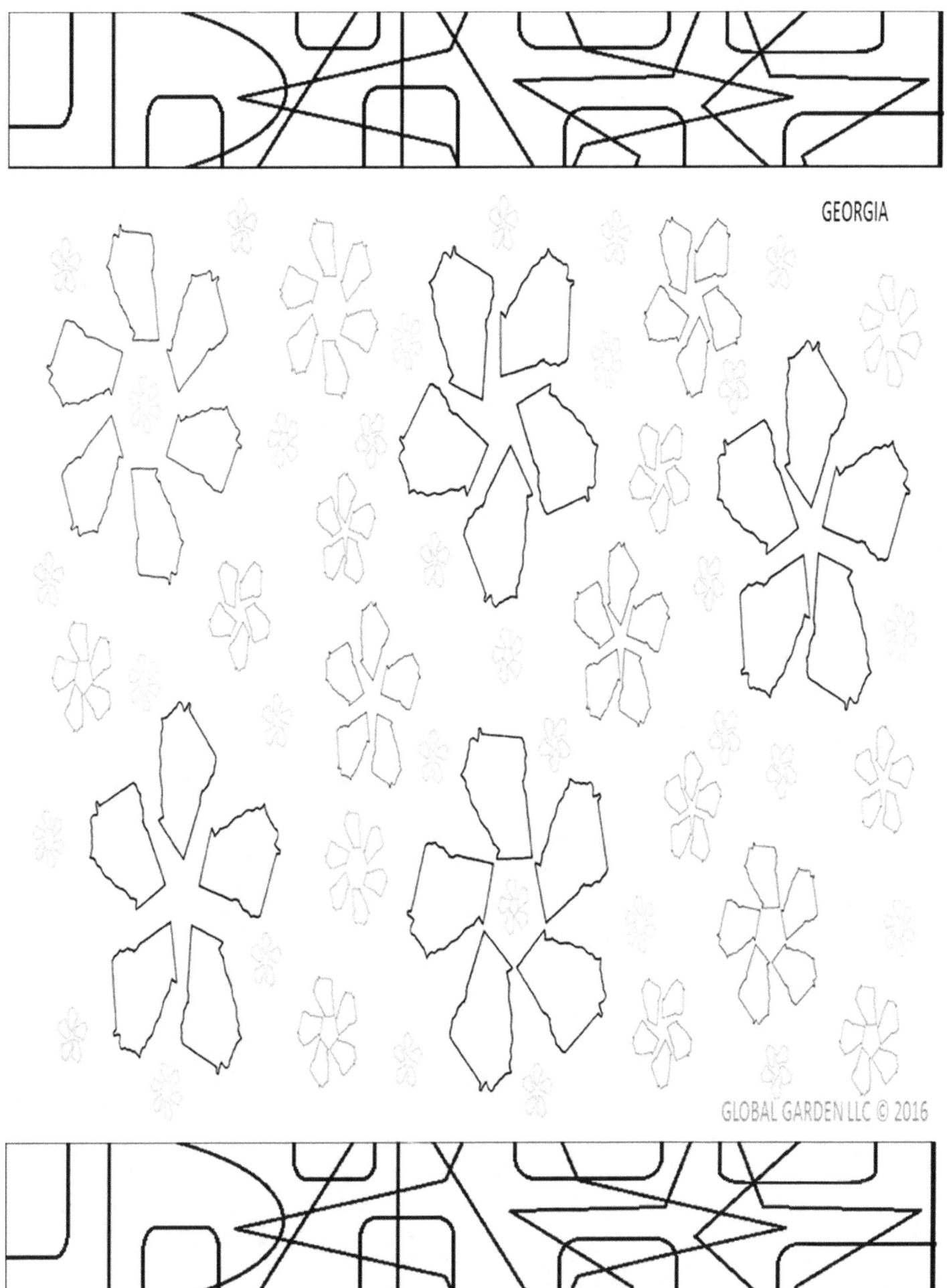

GEORGIA

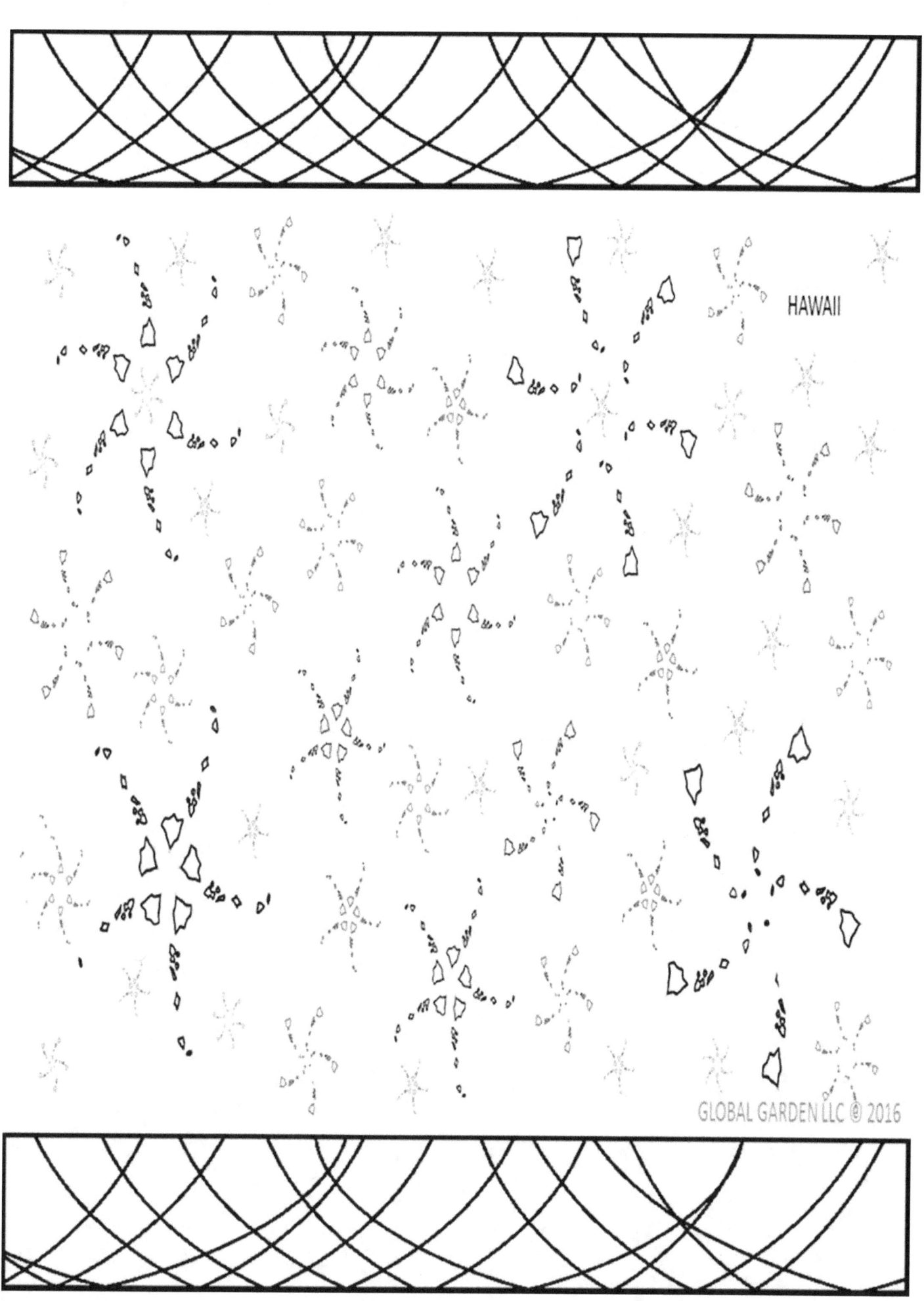

HAWAII

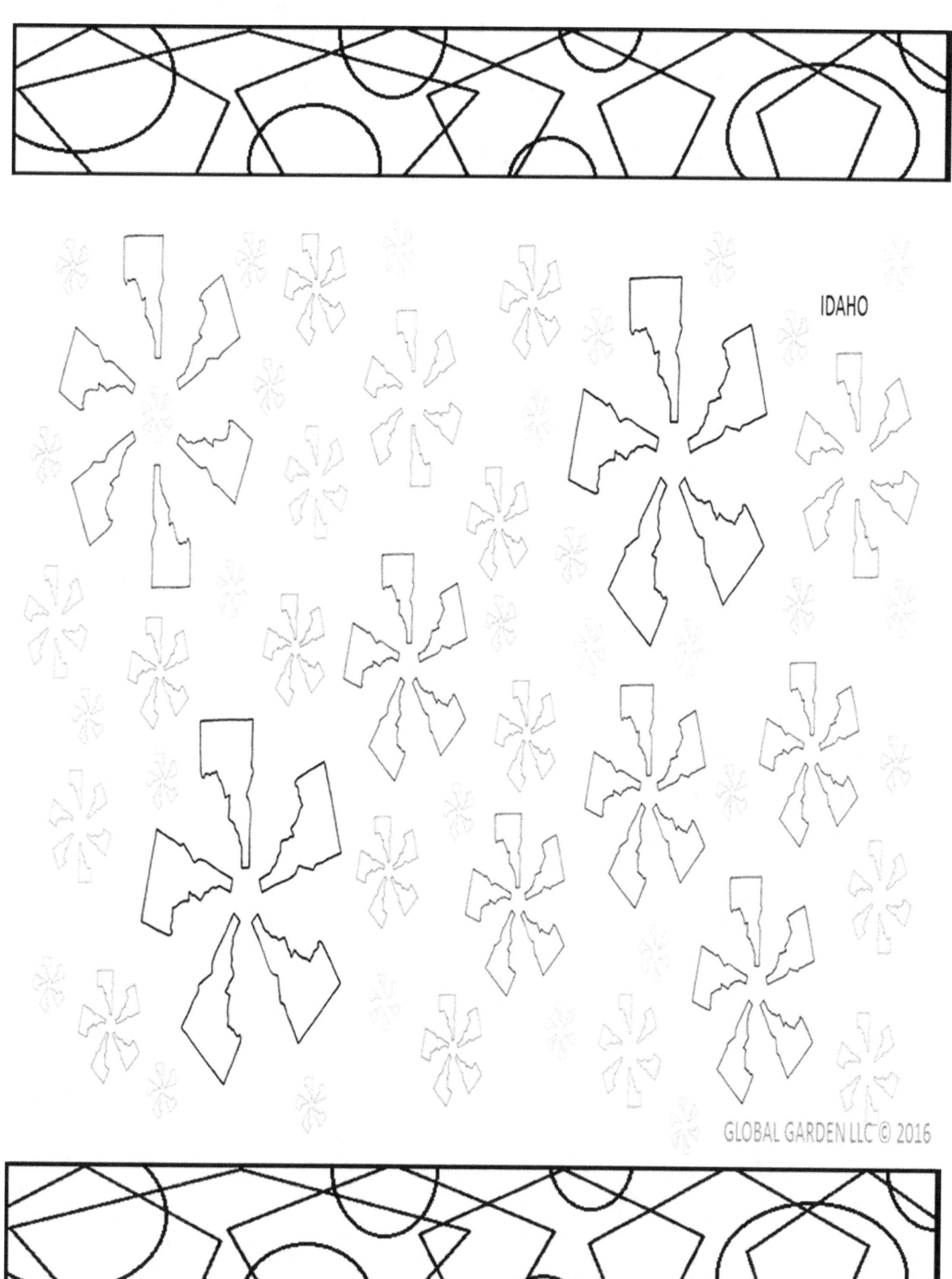

IDAHO

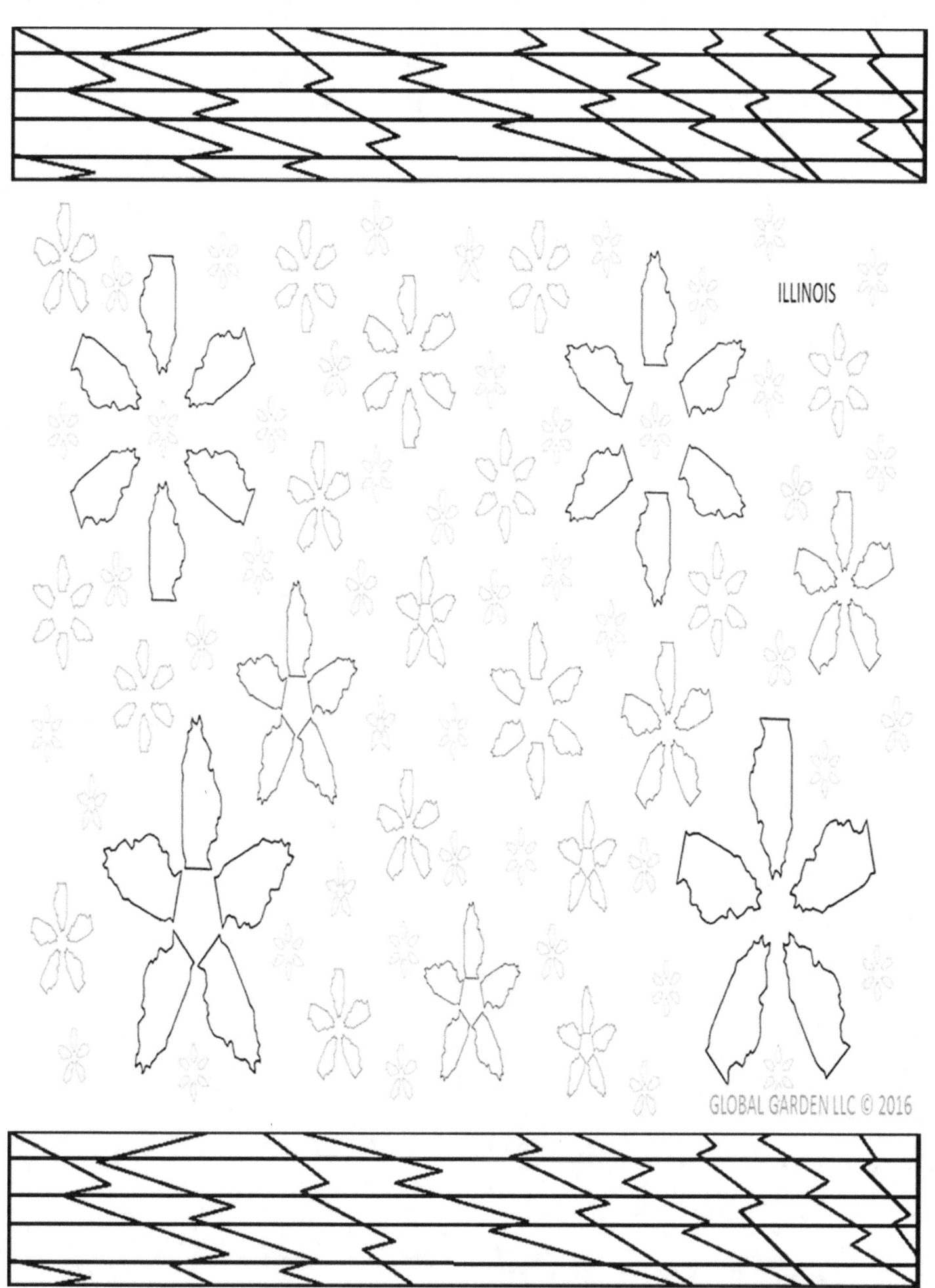

ILLINOIS

INDIANA

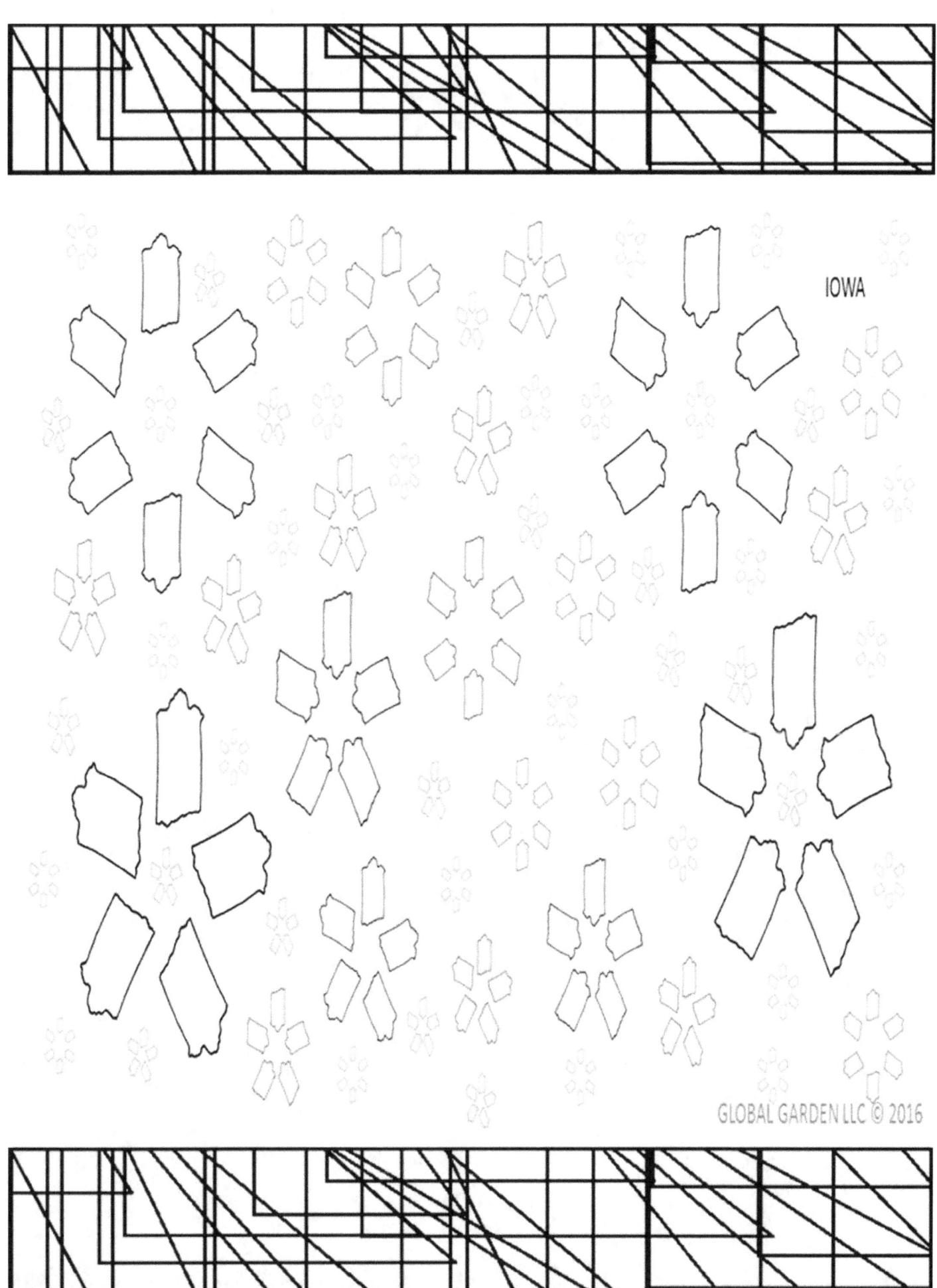

IOWA

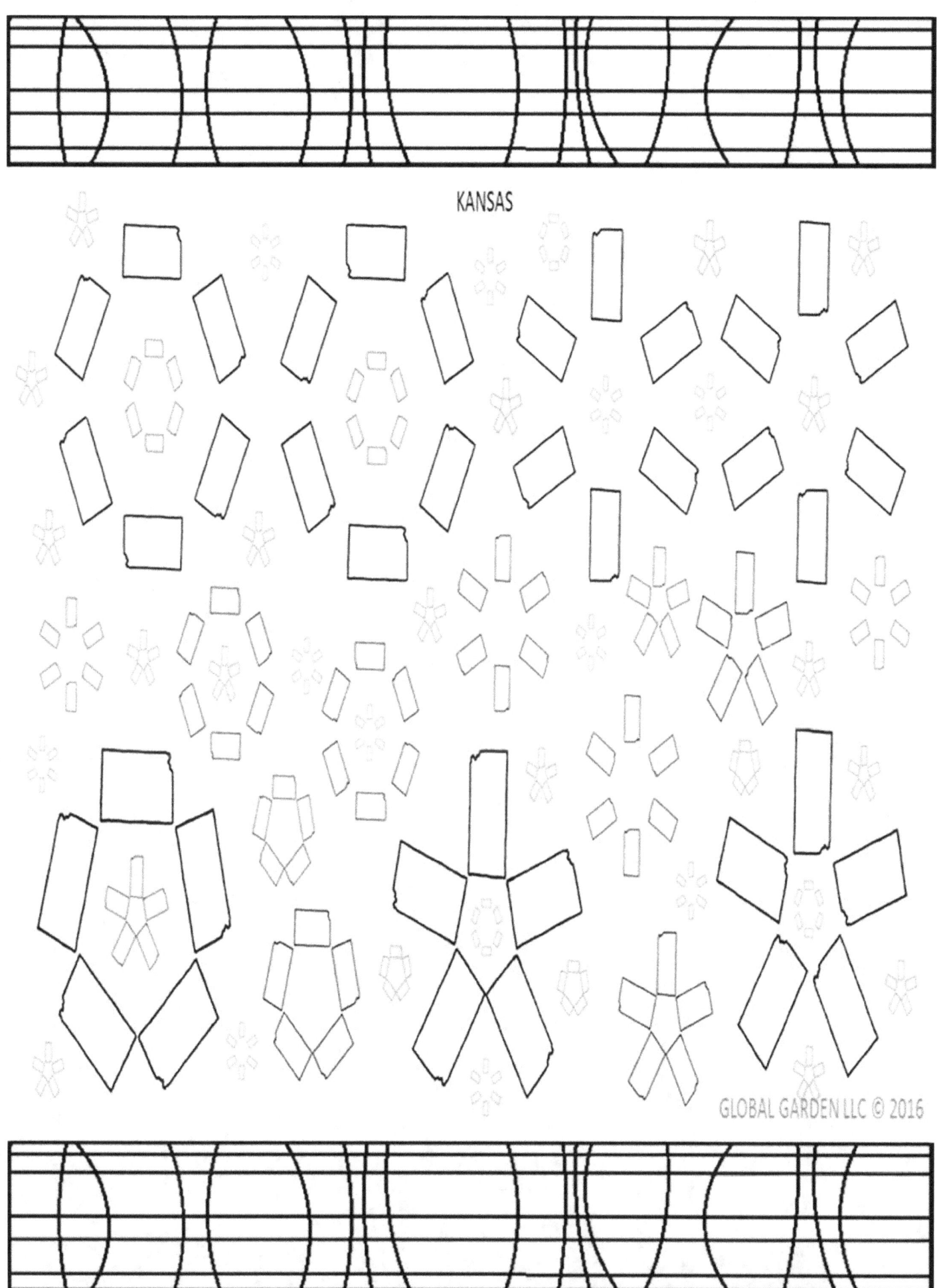

KANSAS

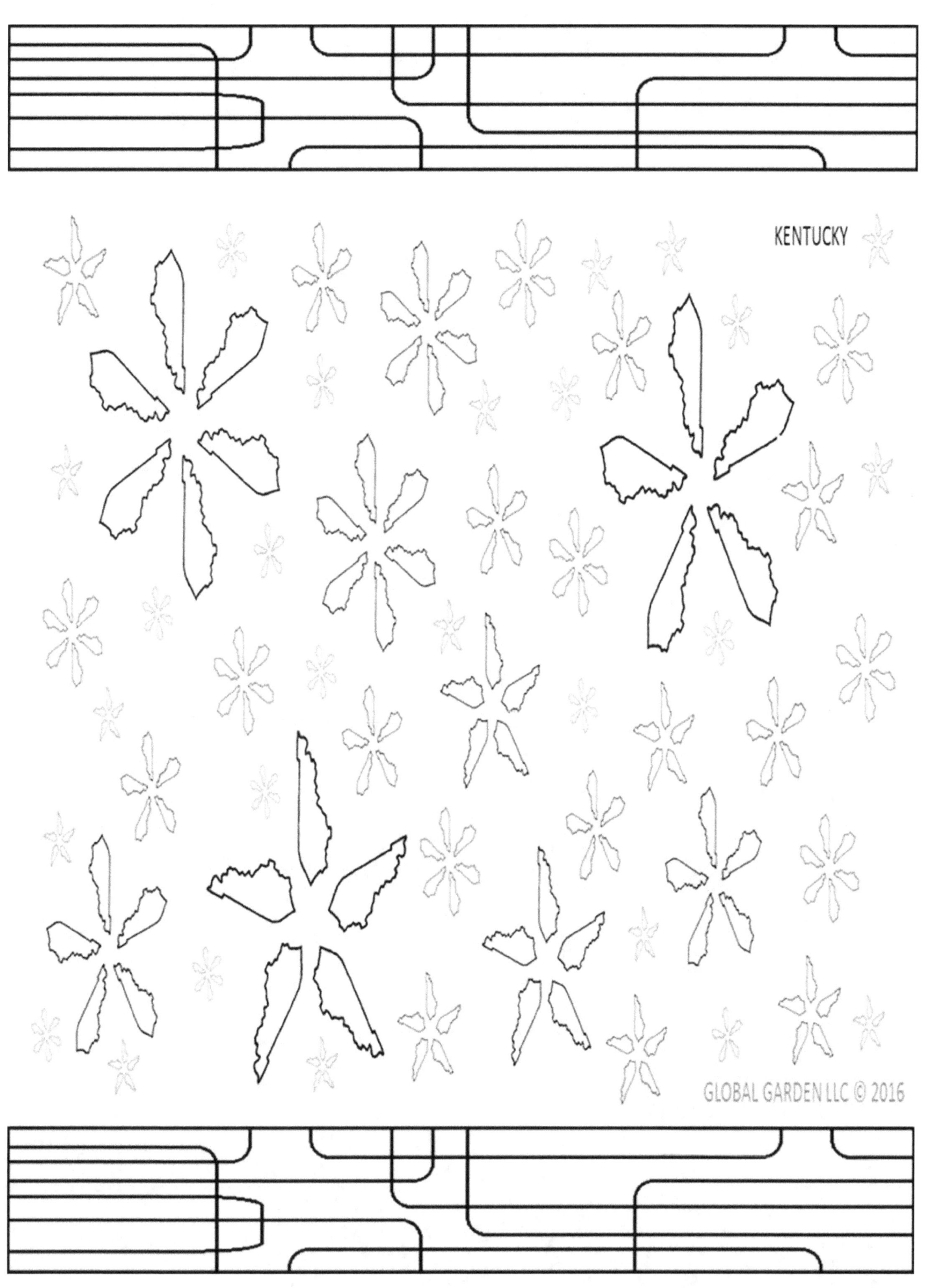

KENTUCKY

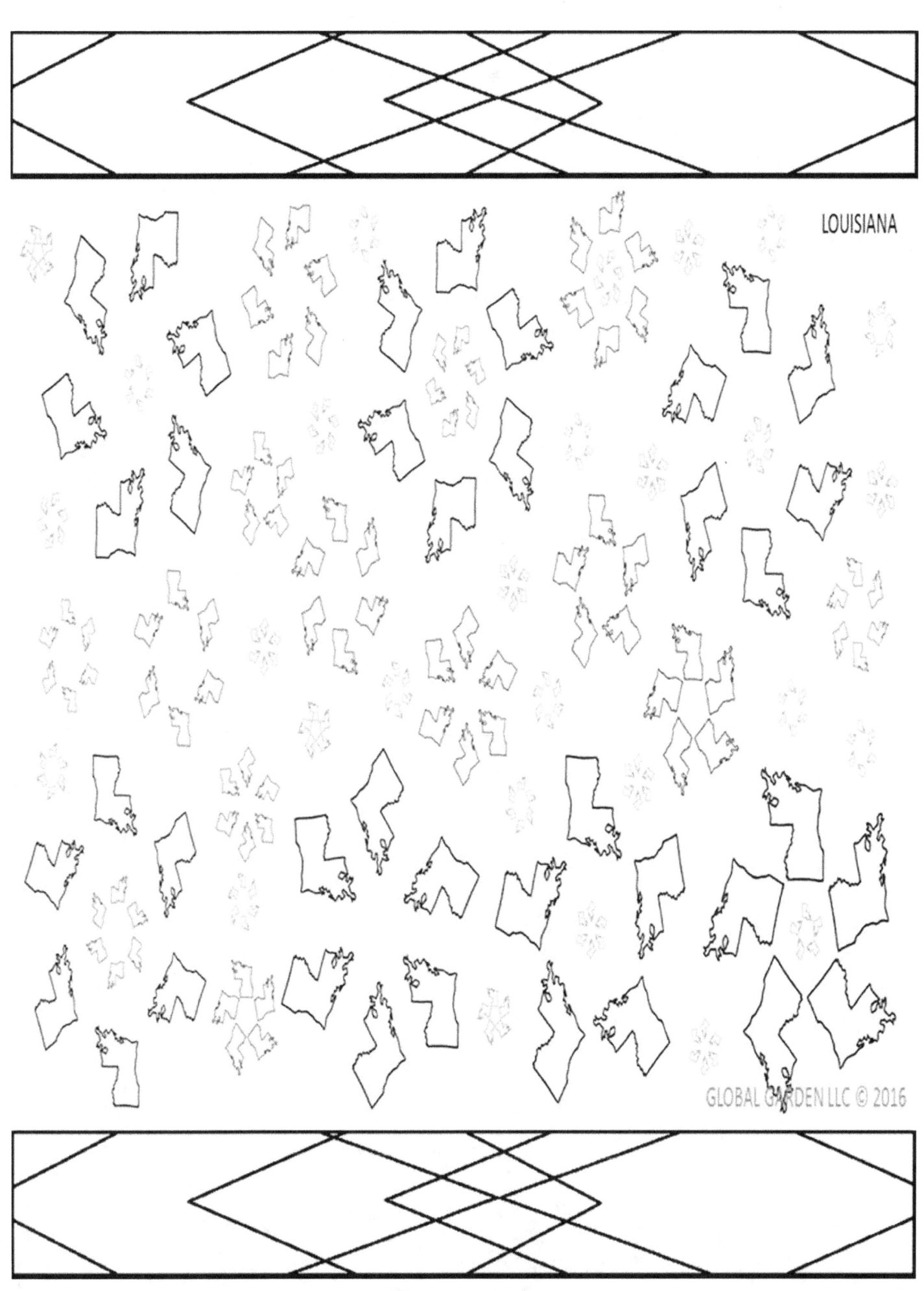

LOUISIANA

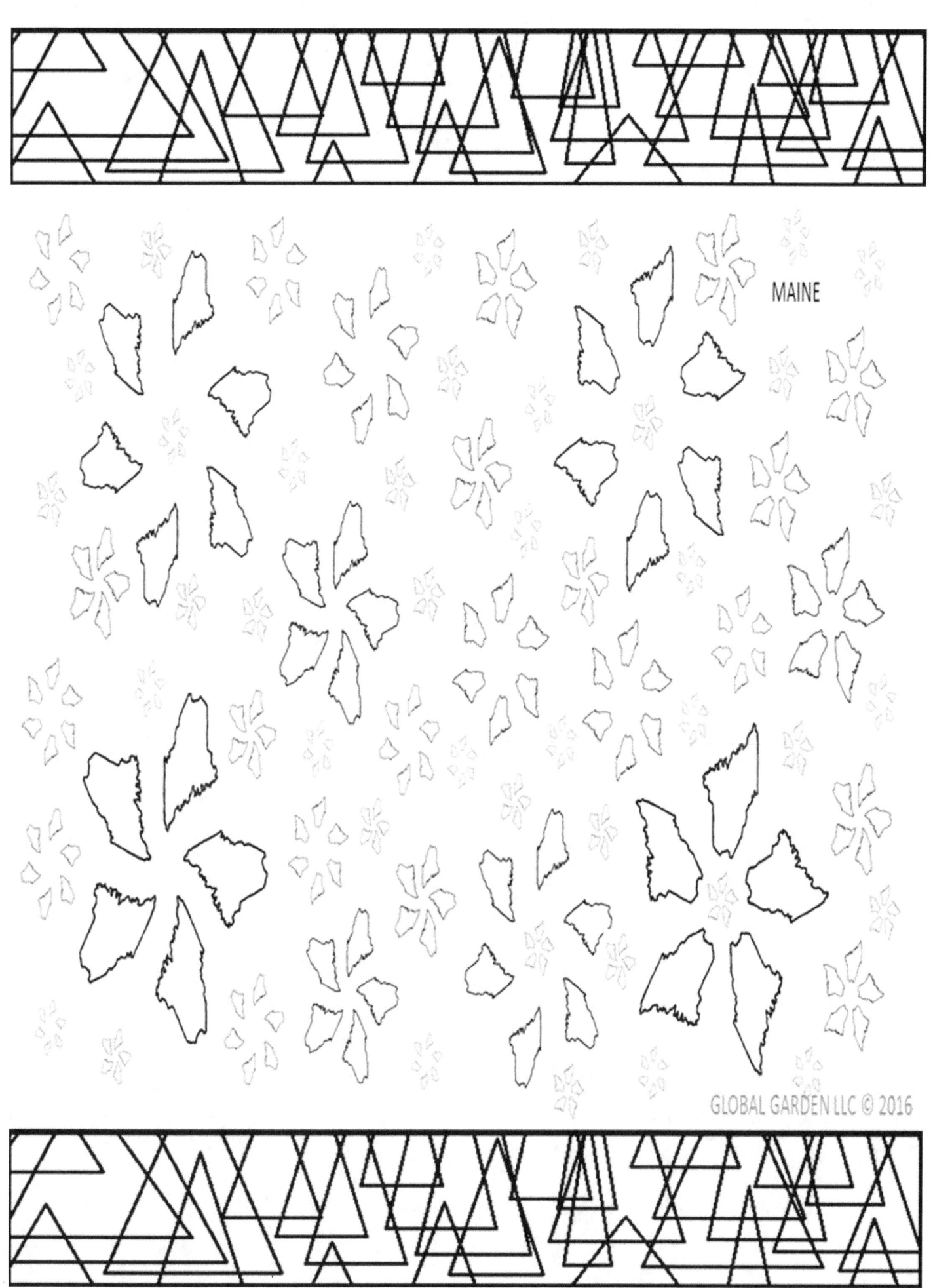

MAINE

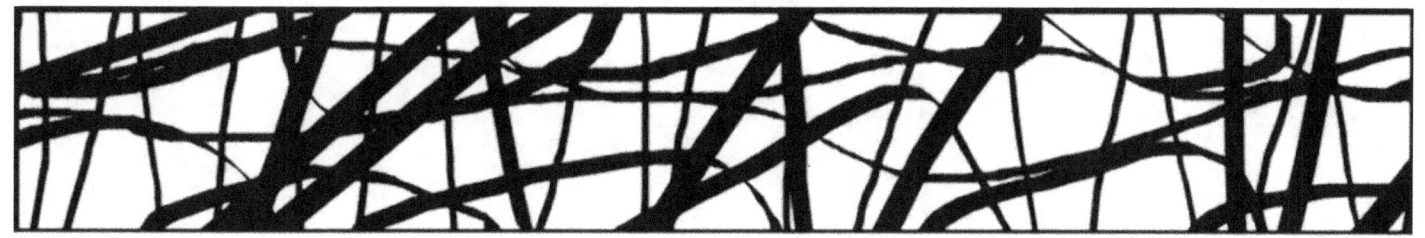

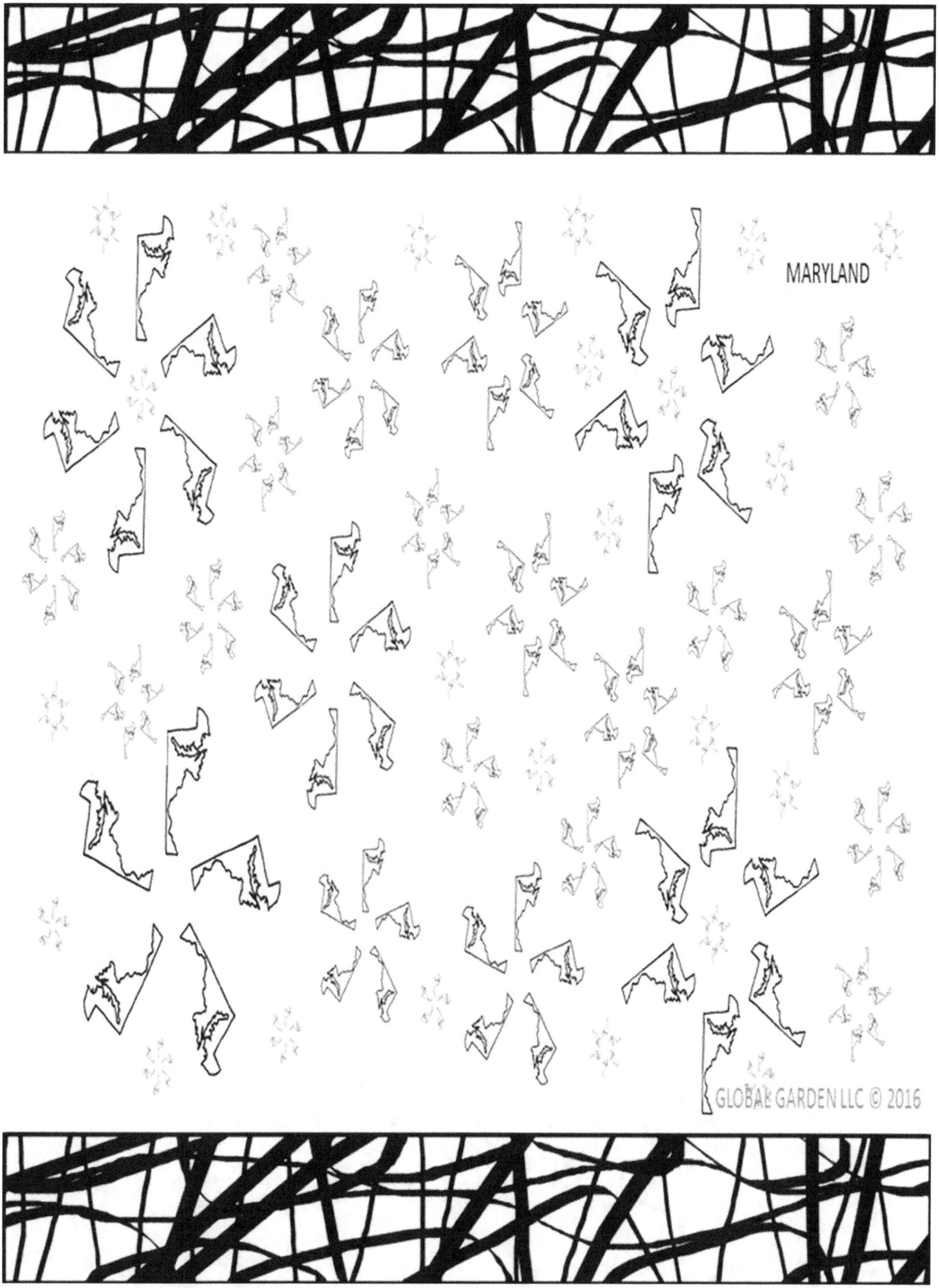

MARYLAND

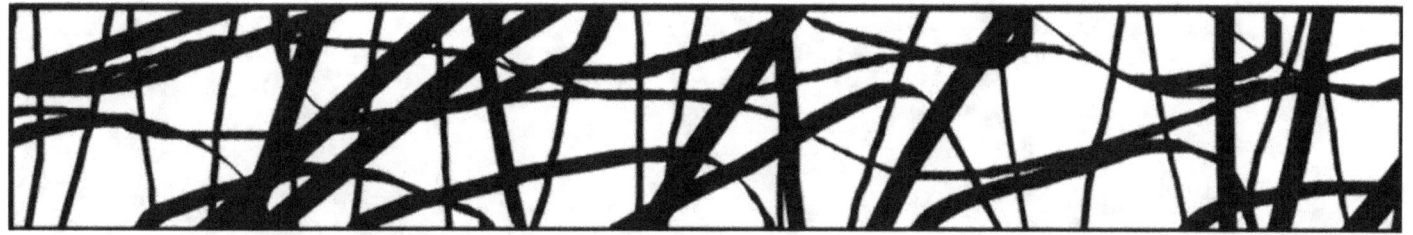

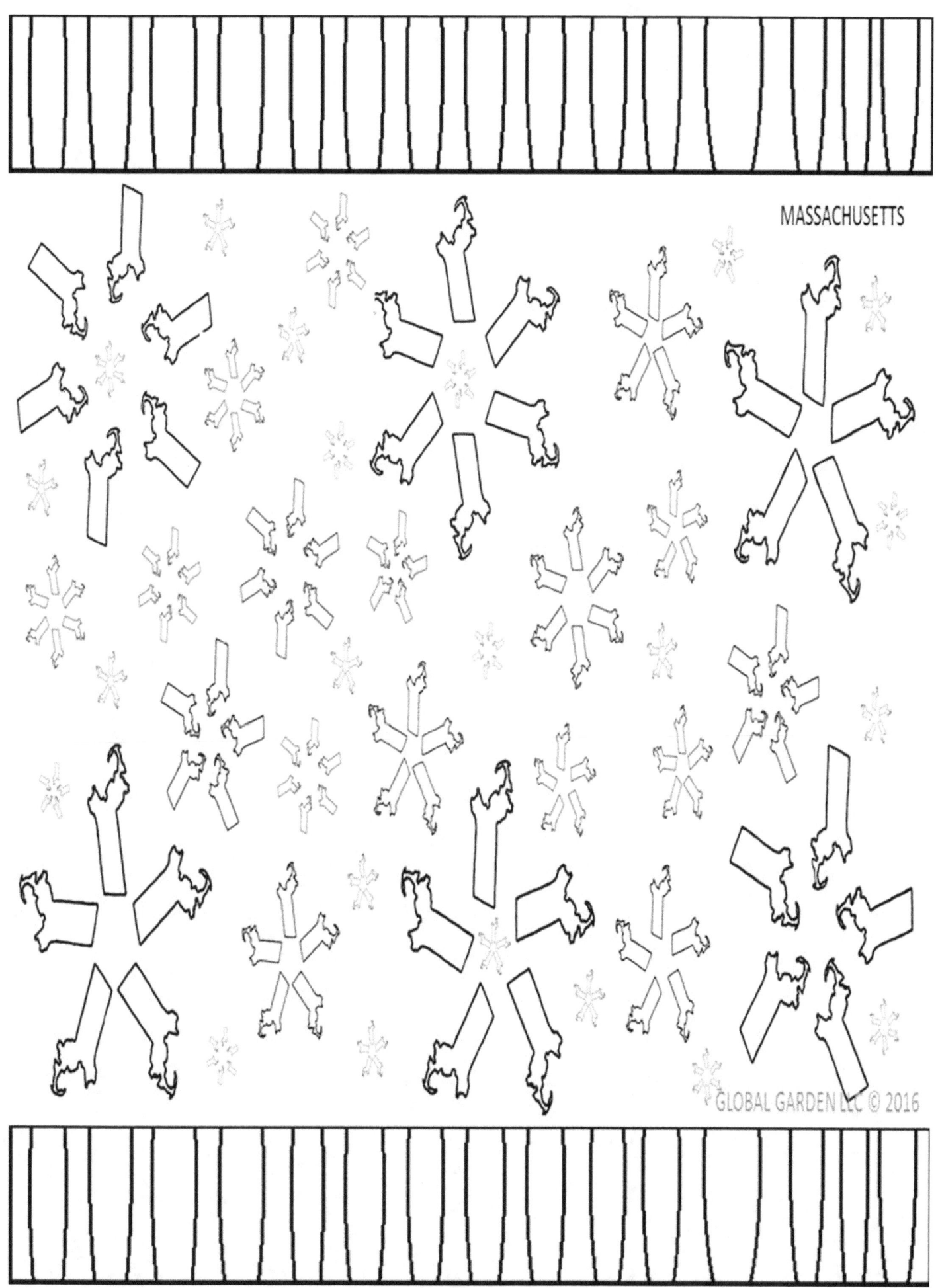

MASSACHUSETTS

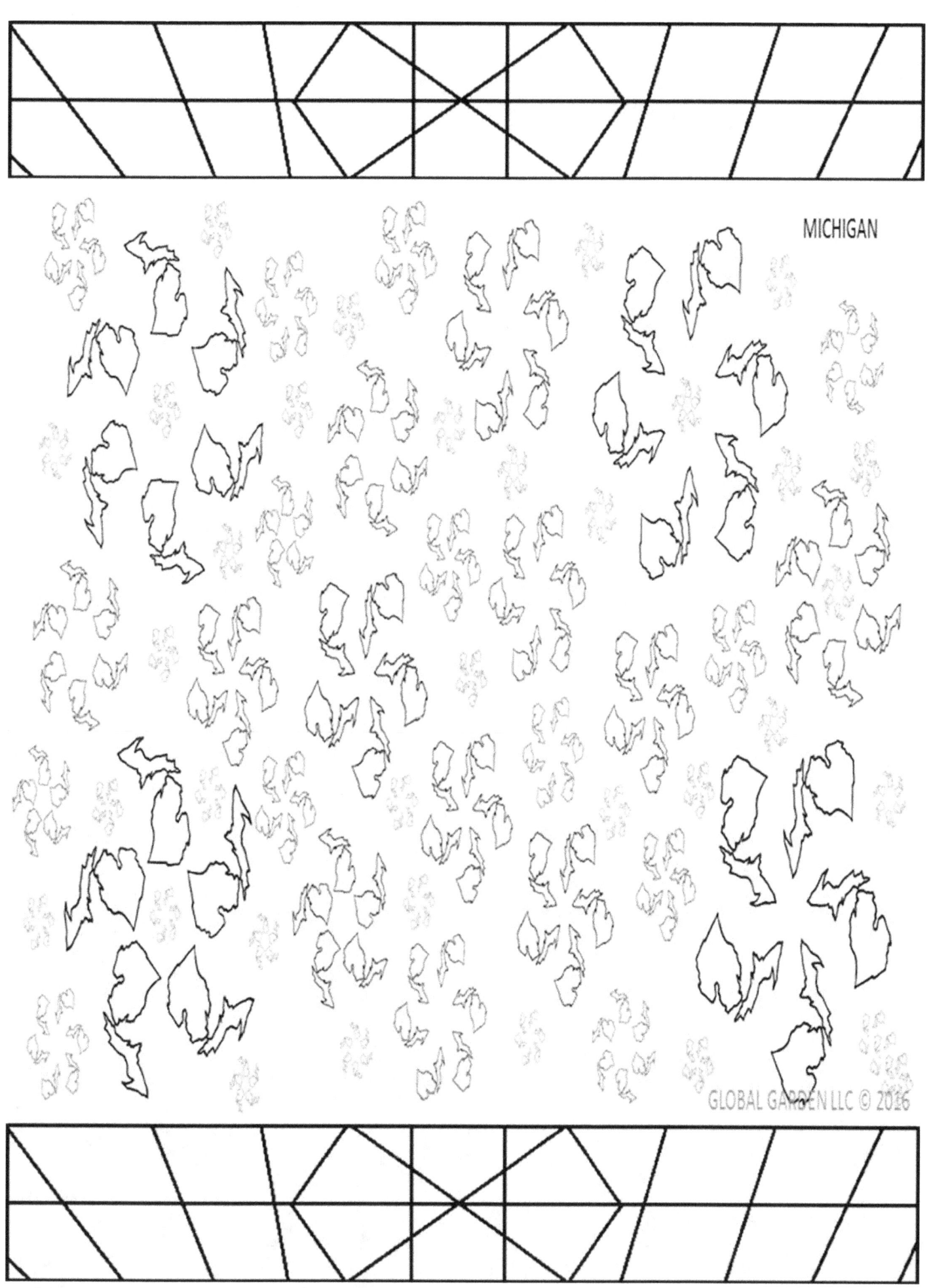

MICHIGAN

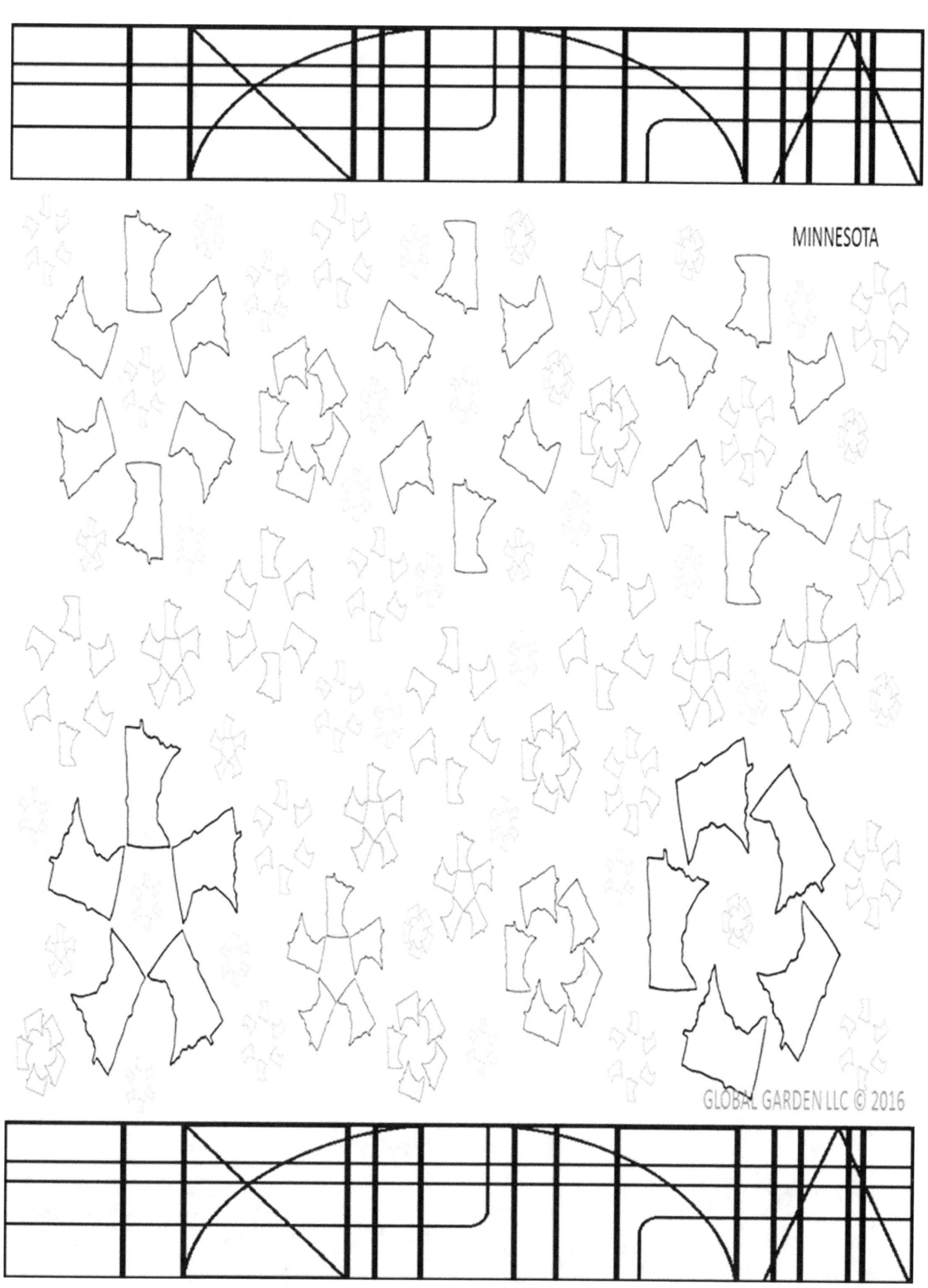

MINNESOTA

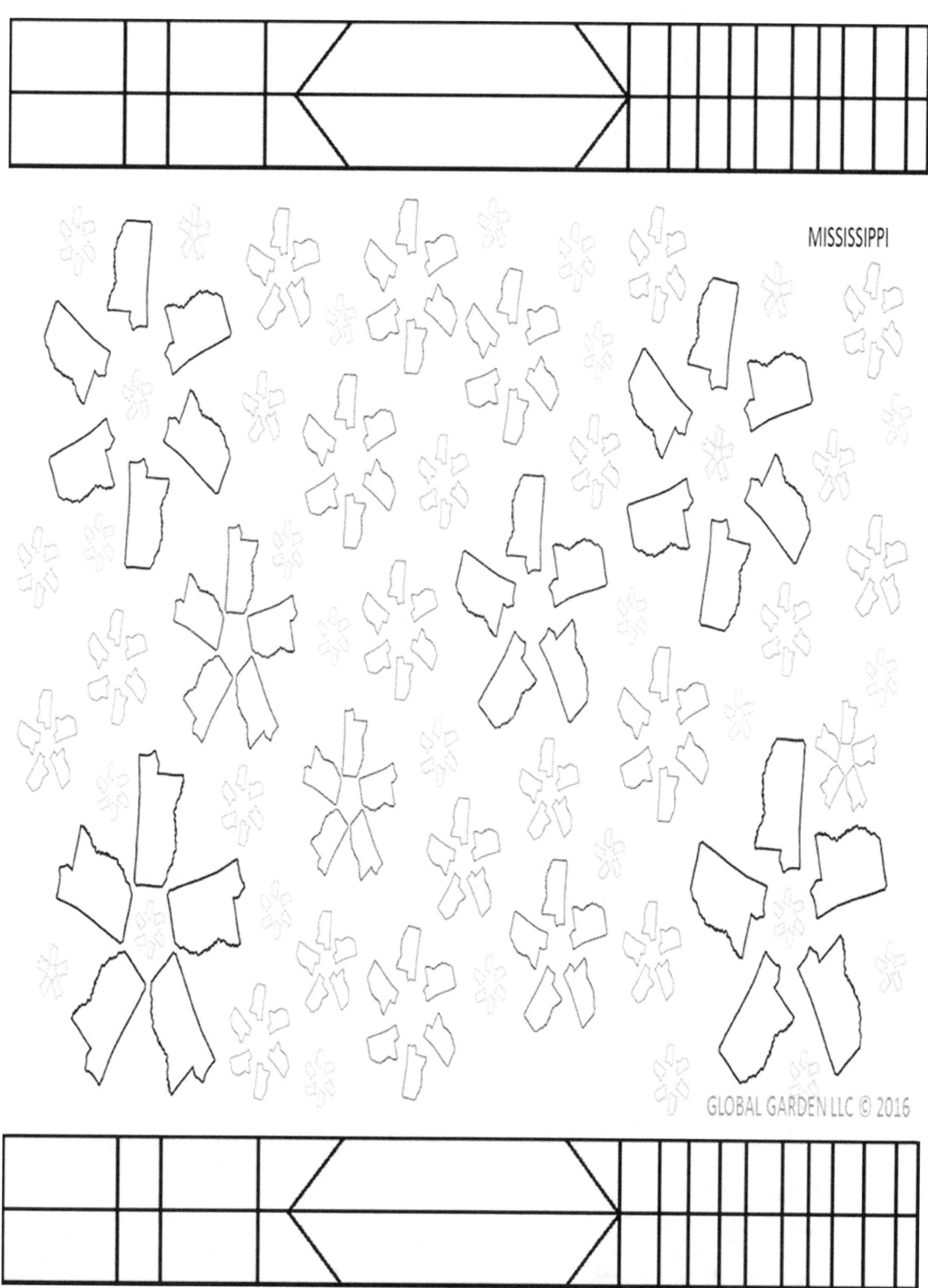

MISSISSIPPI

GLOBAL GARDEN LLC © 2016

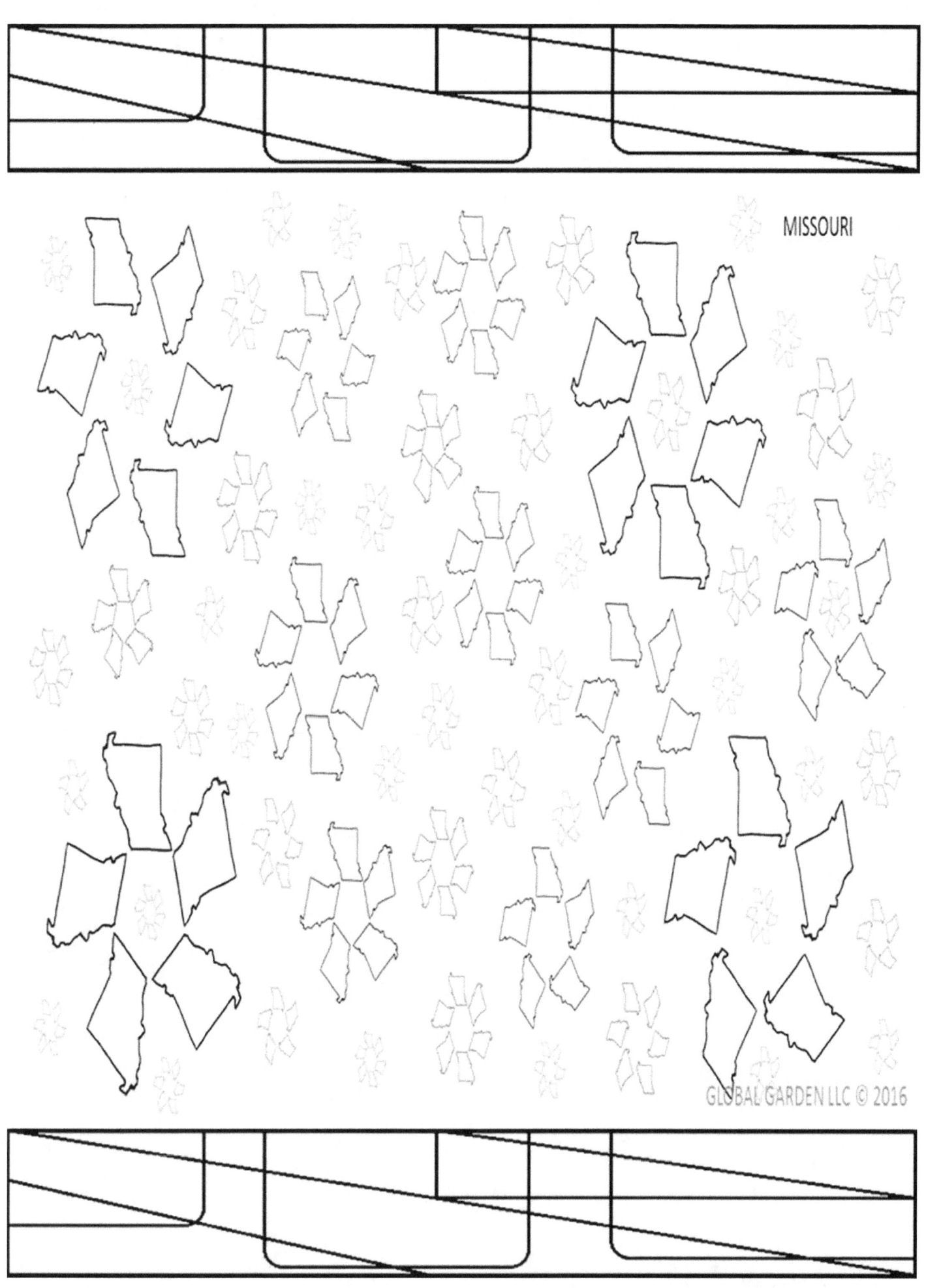

MISSOURI

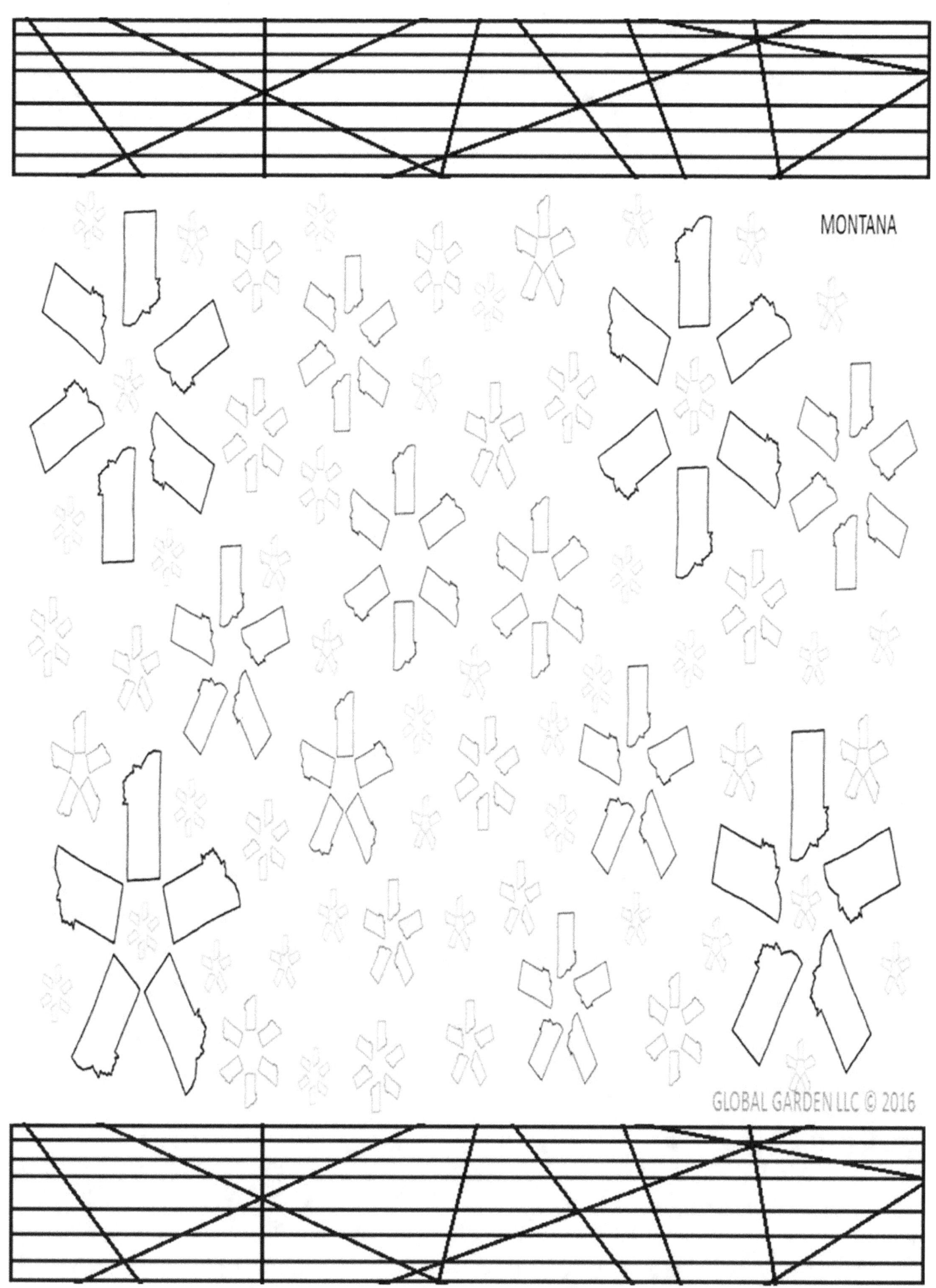

MONTANA

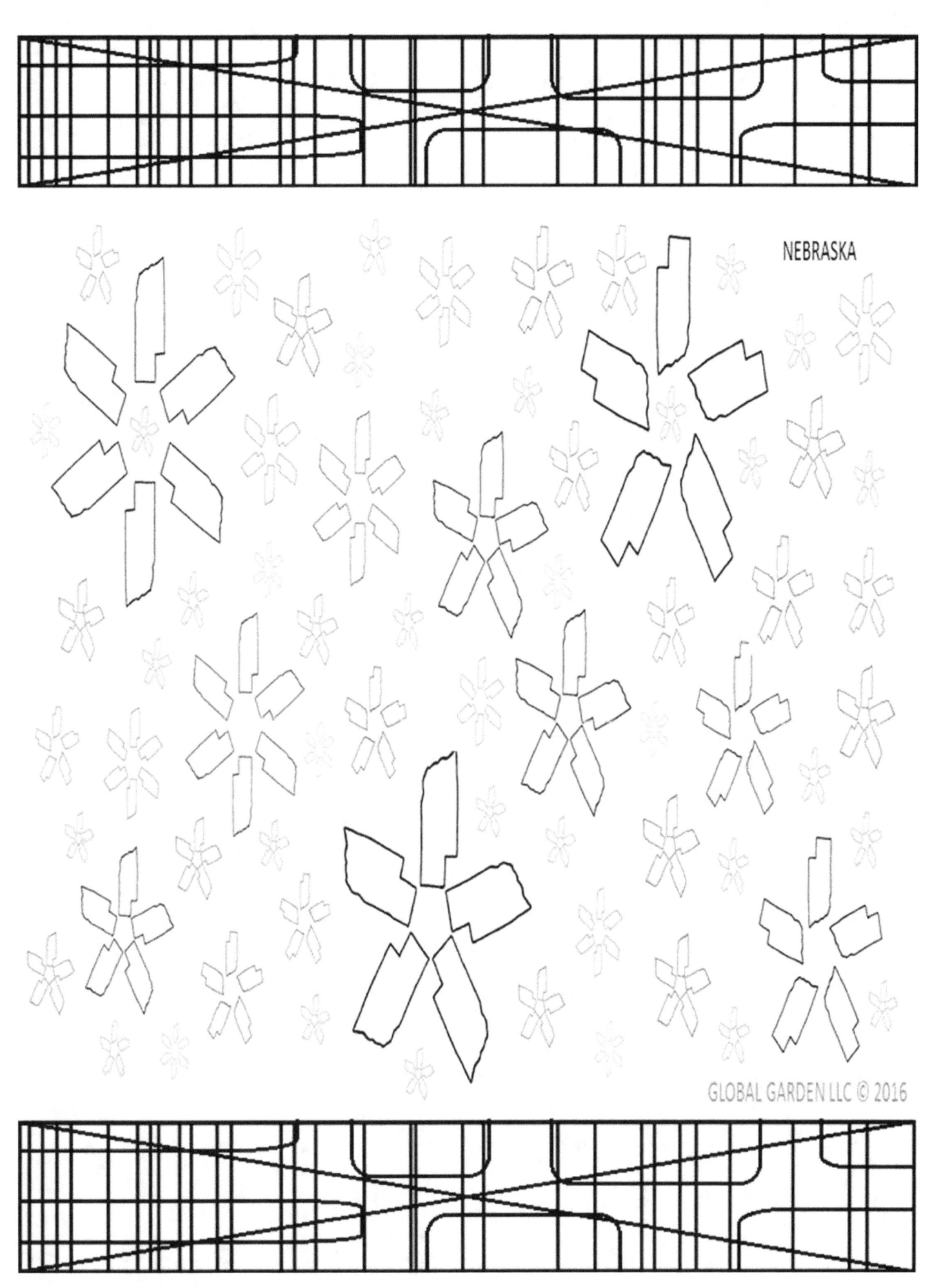

NEBRASKA

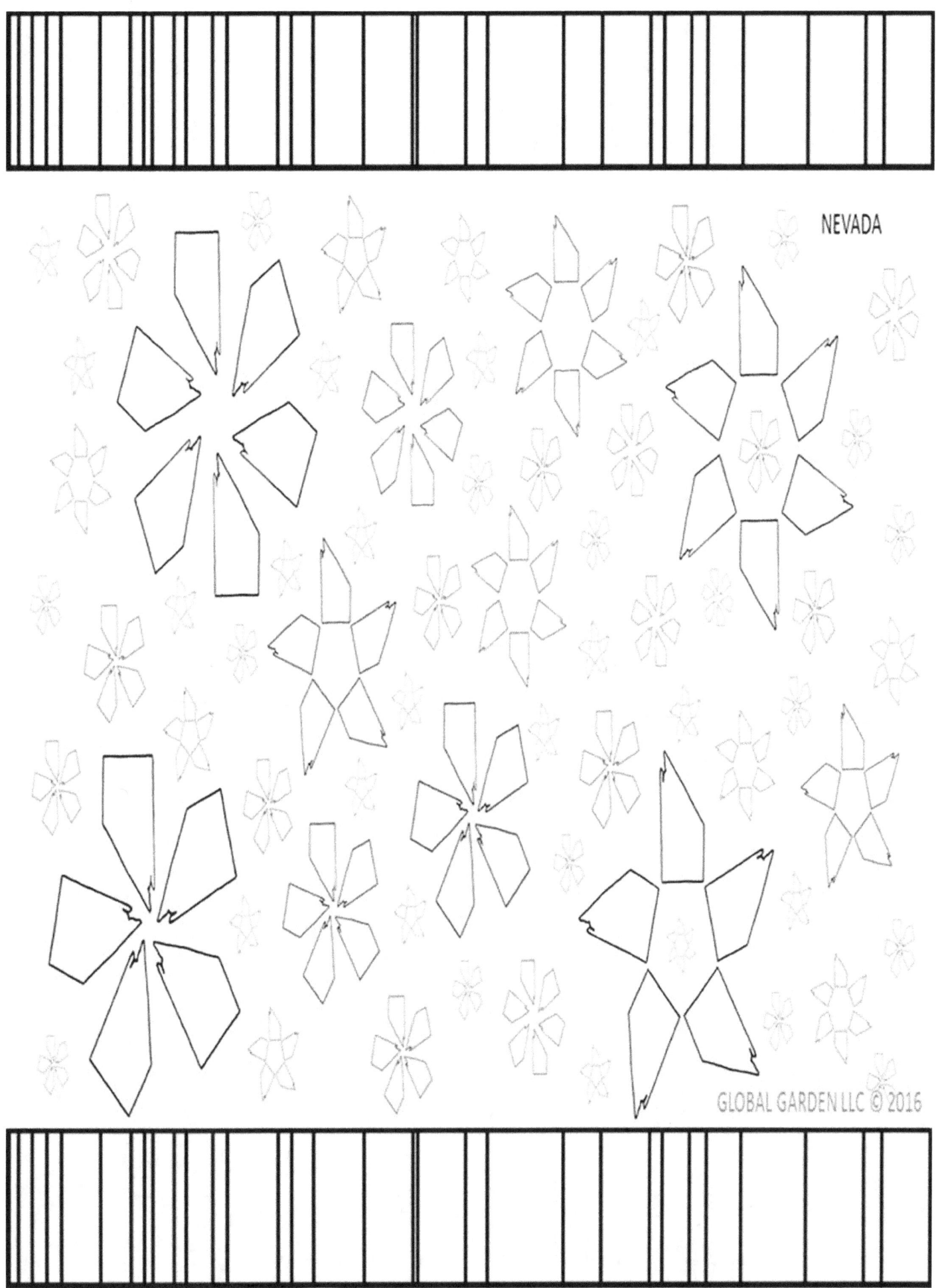

NEVADA

NEW HAMPSHIRE

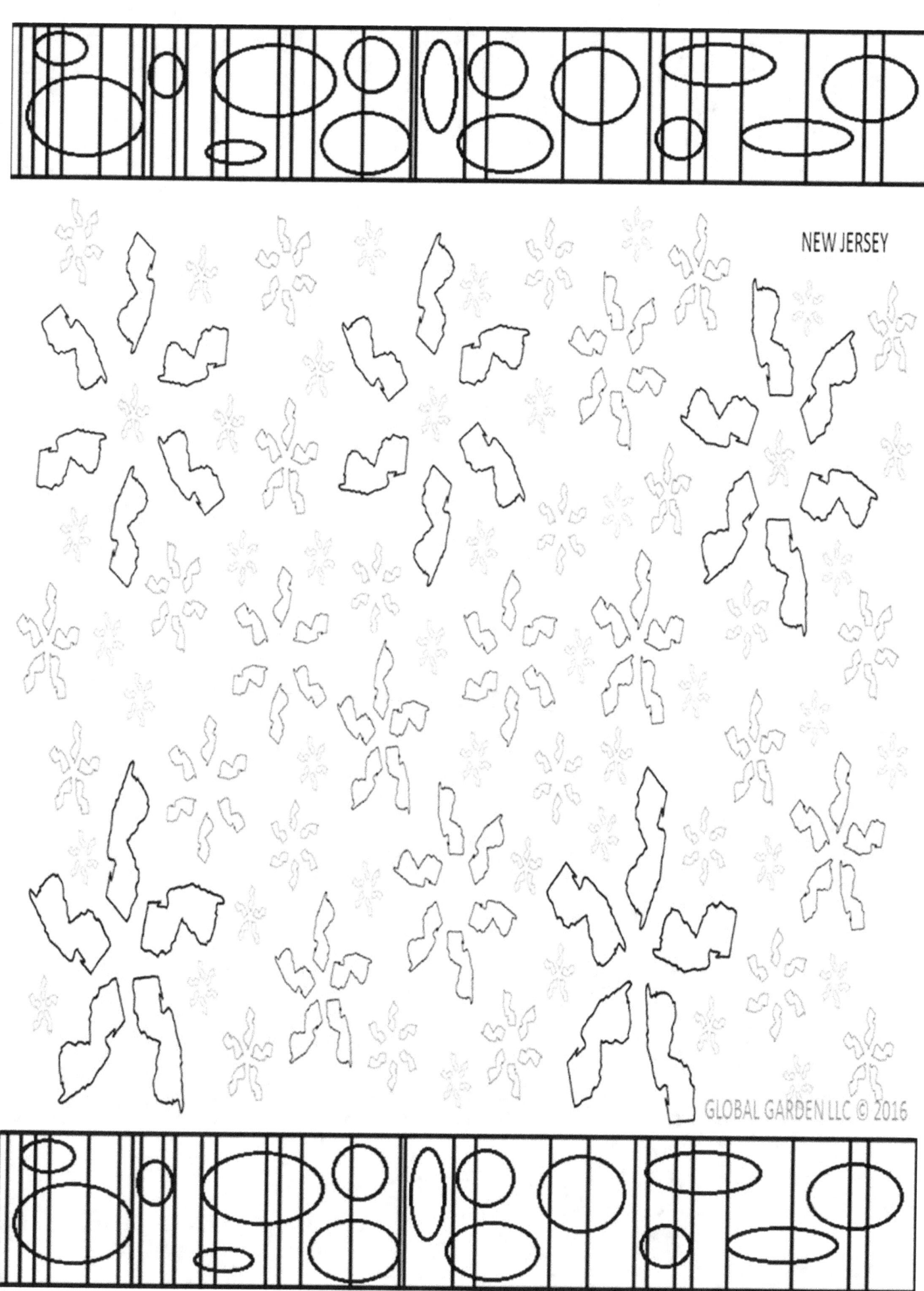

NEW JERSEY

GLOBAL GARDEN LLC © 2016

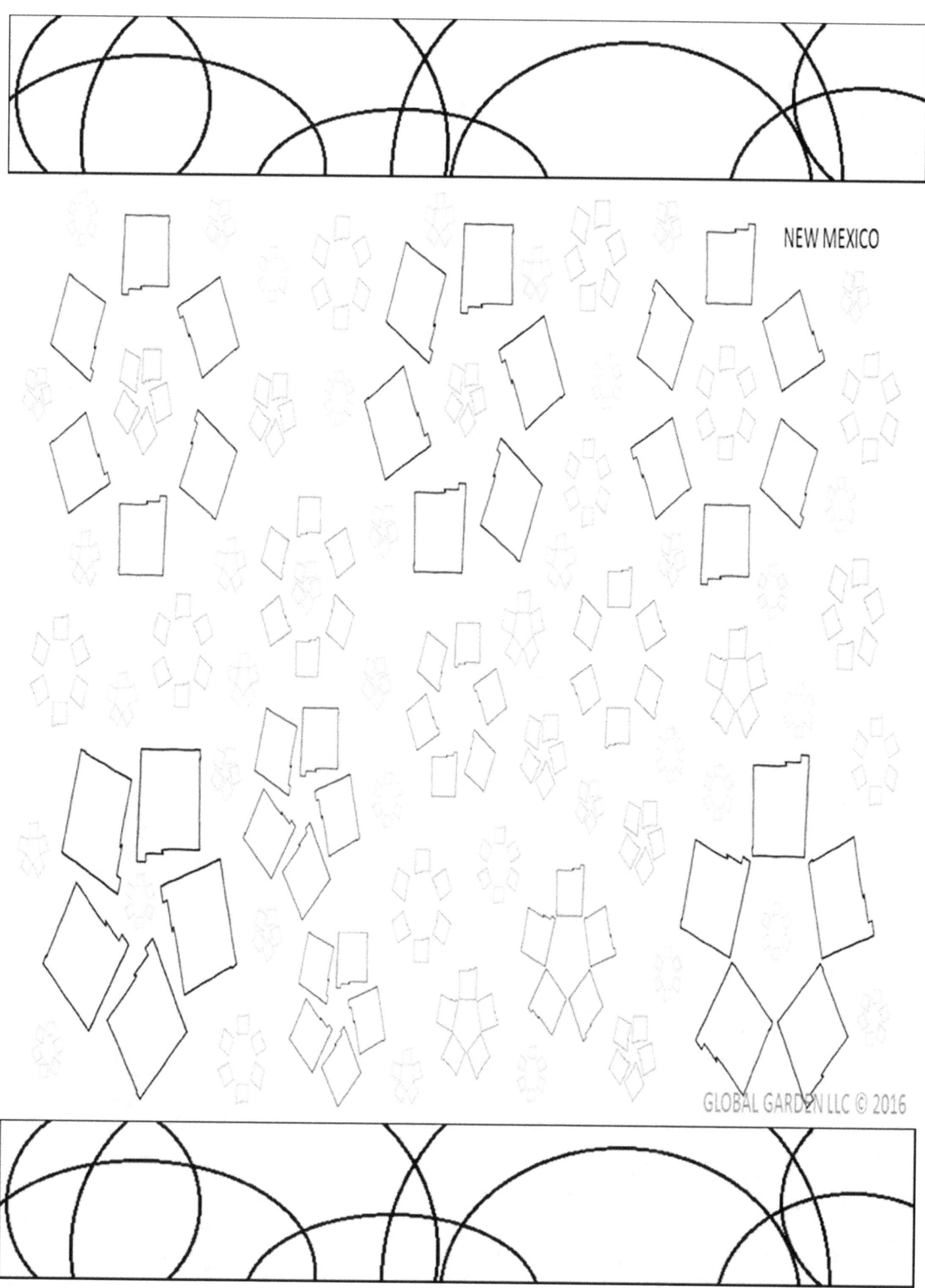

NEW MEXICO

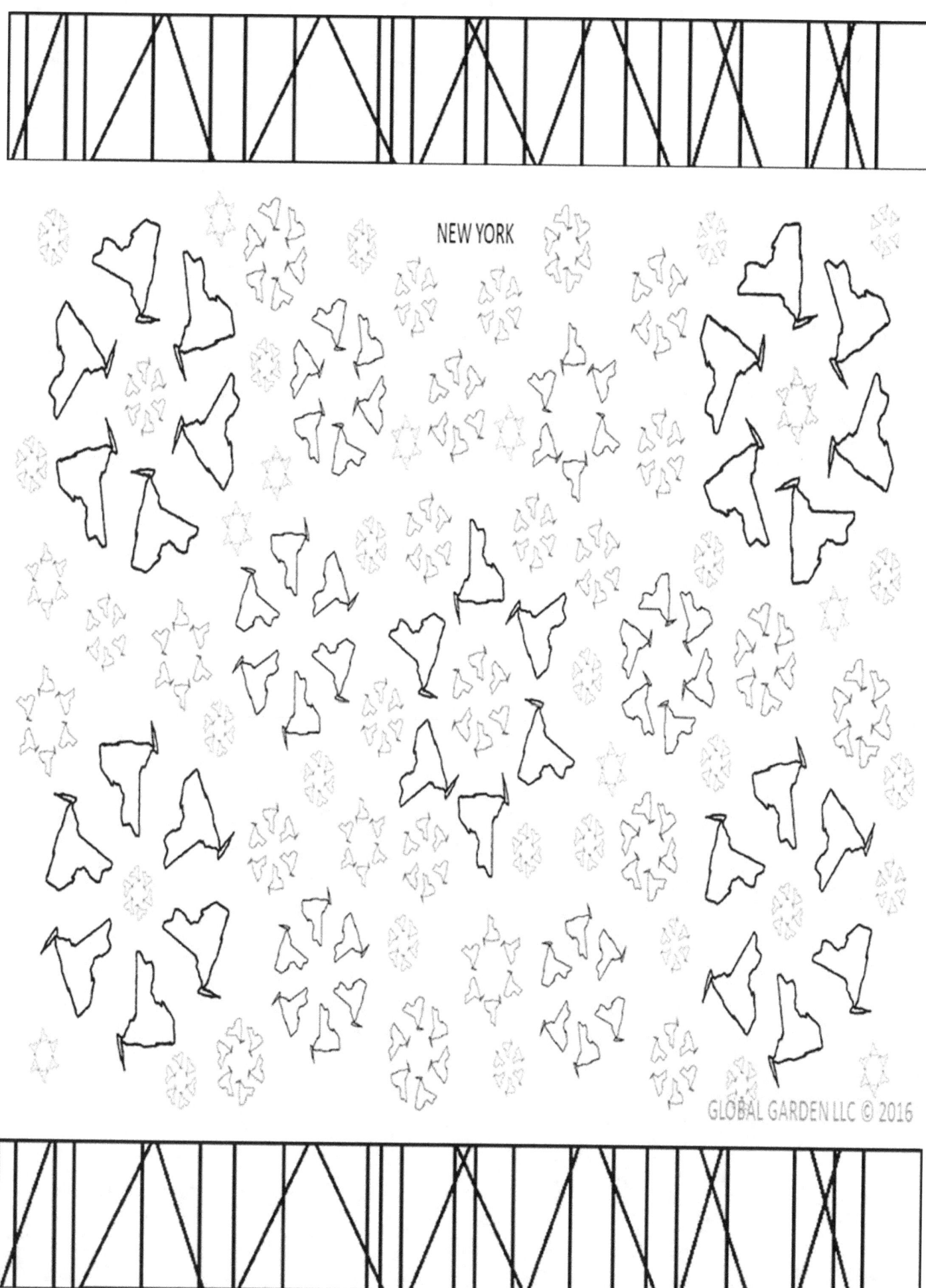

NEW YORK

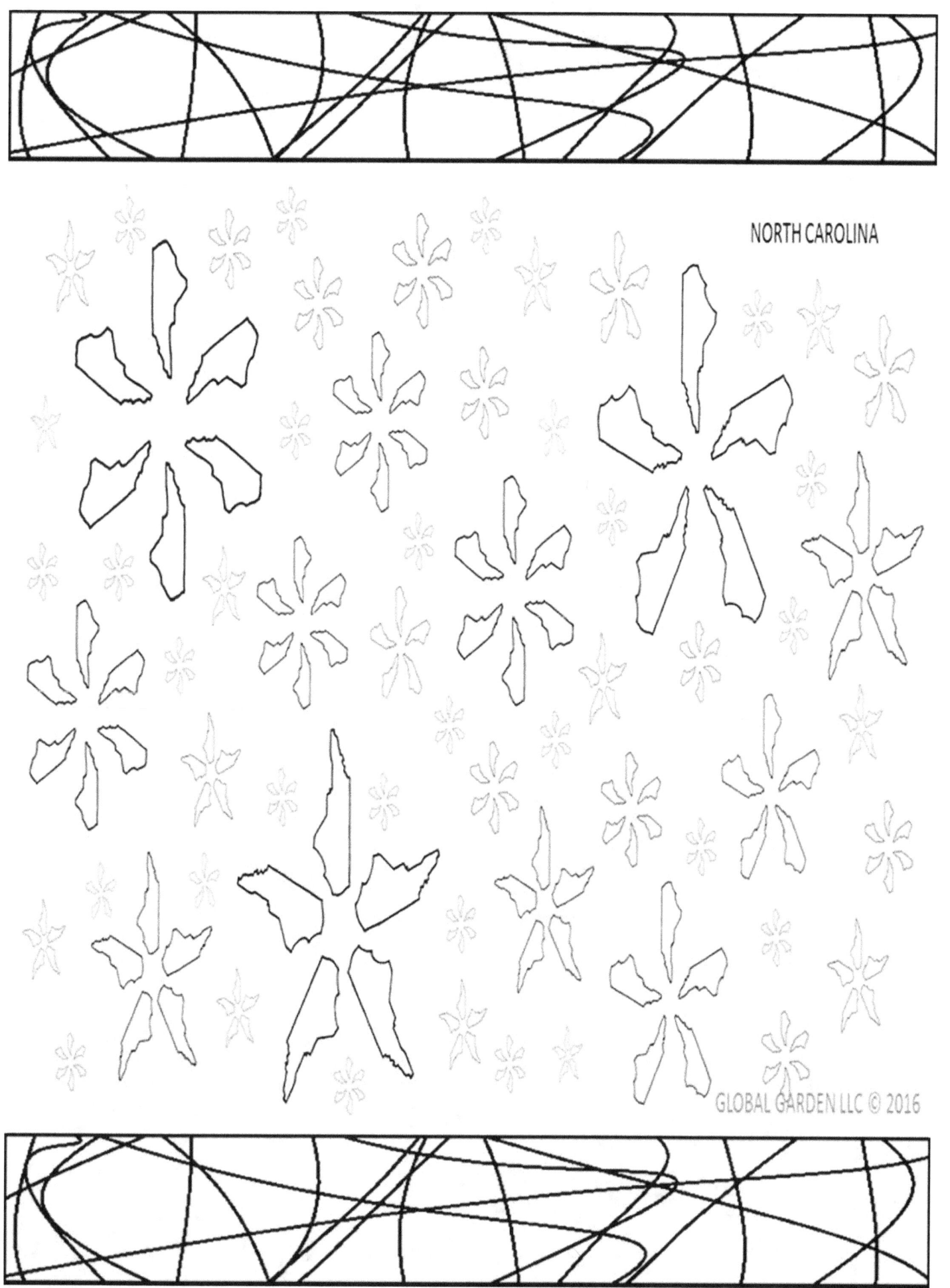

NORTH CAROLINA

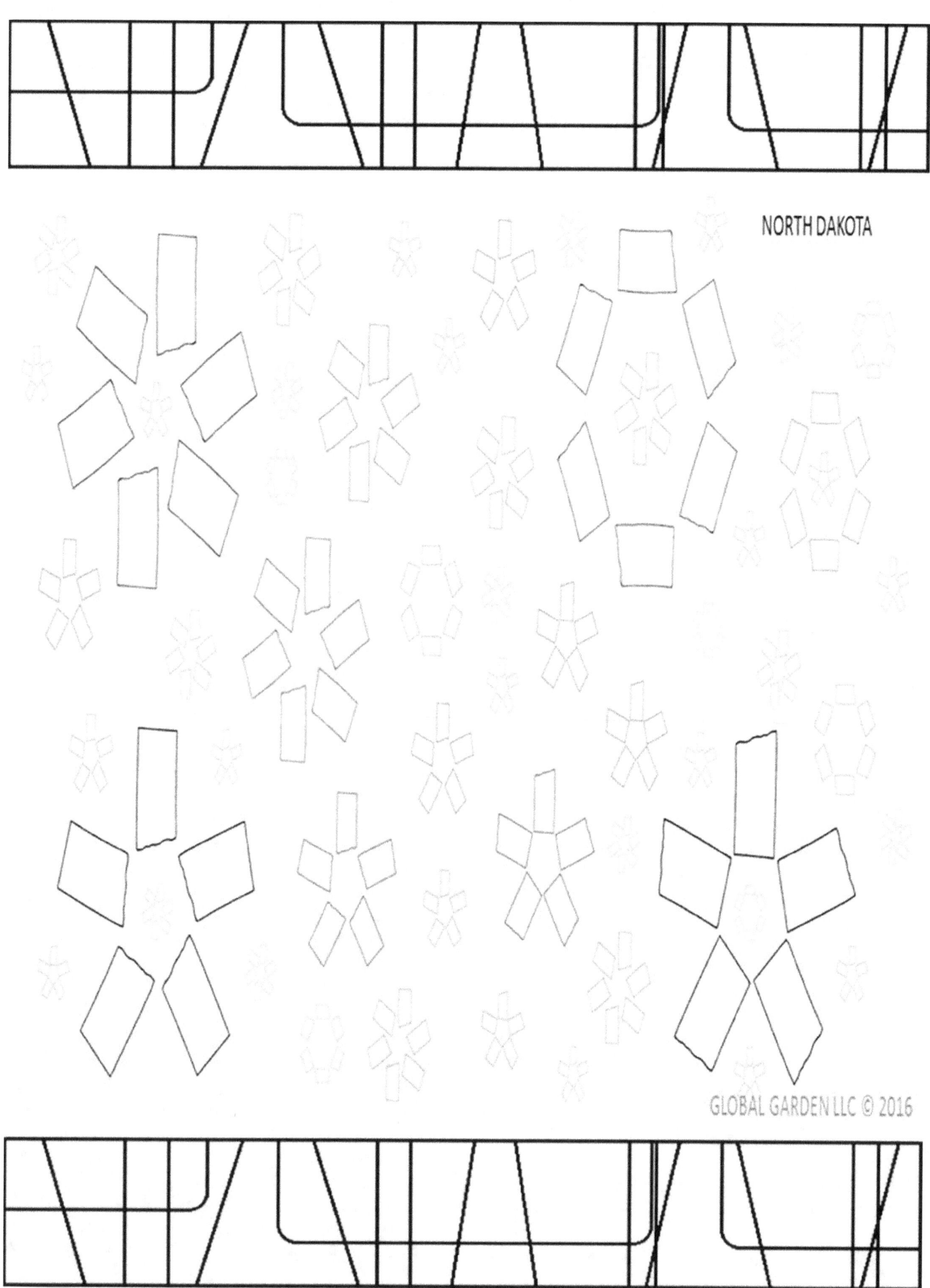

NORTH DAKOTA

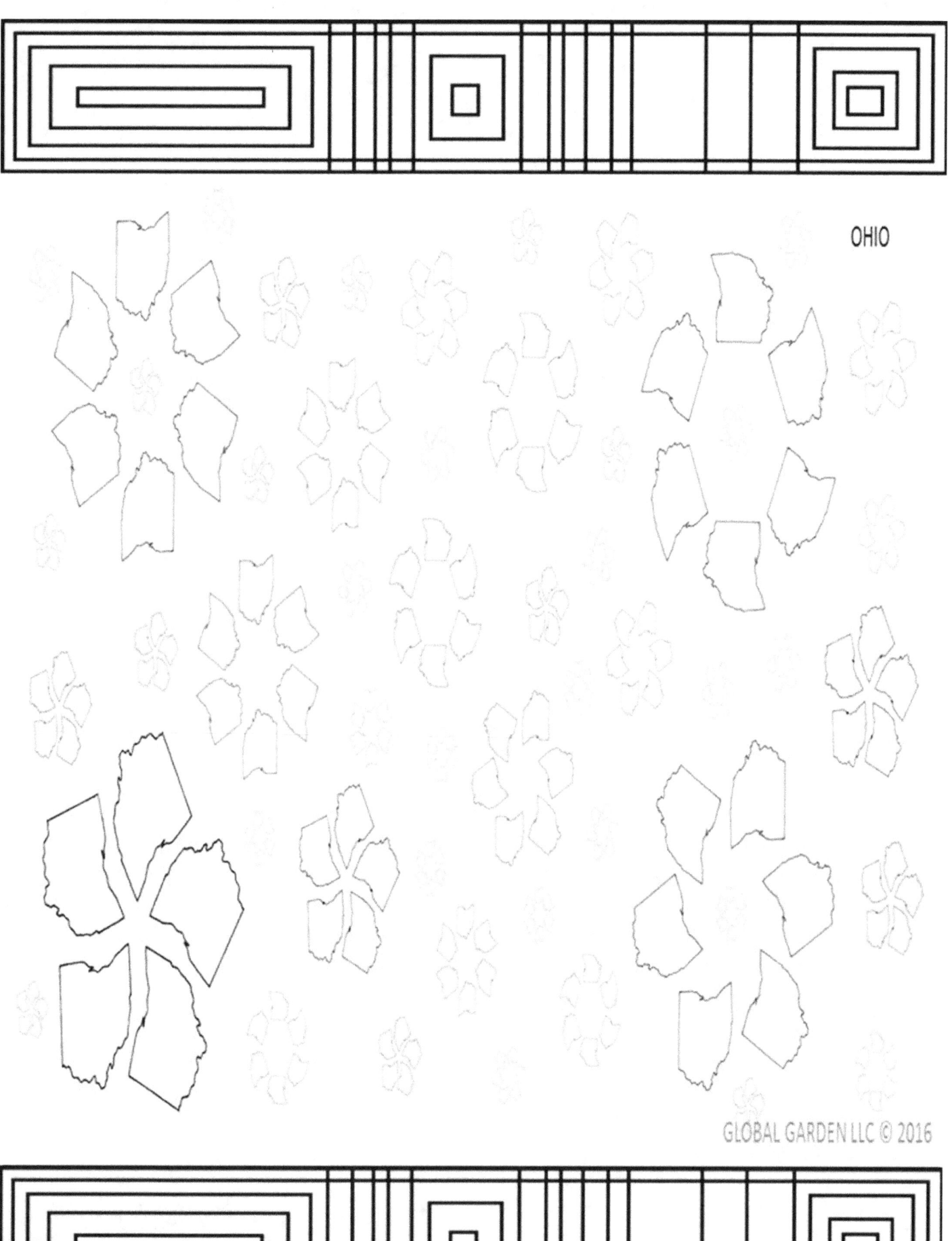

OHIO

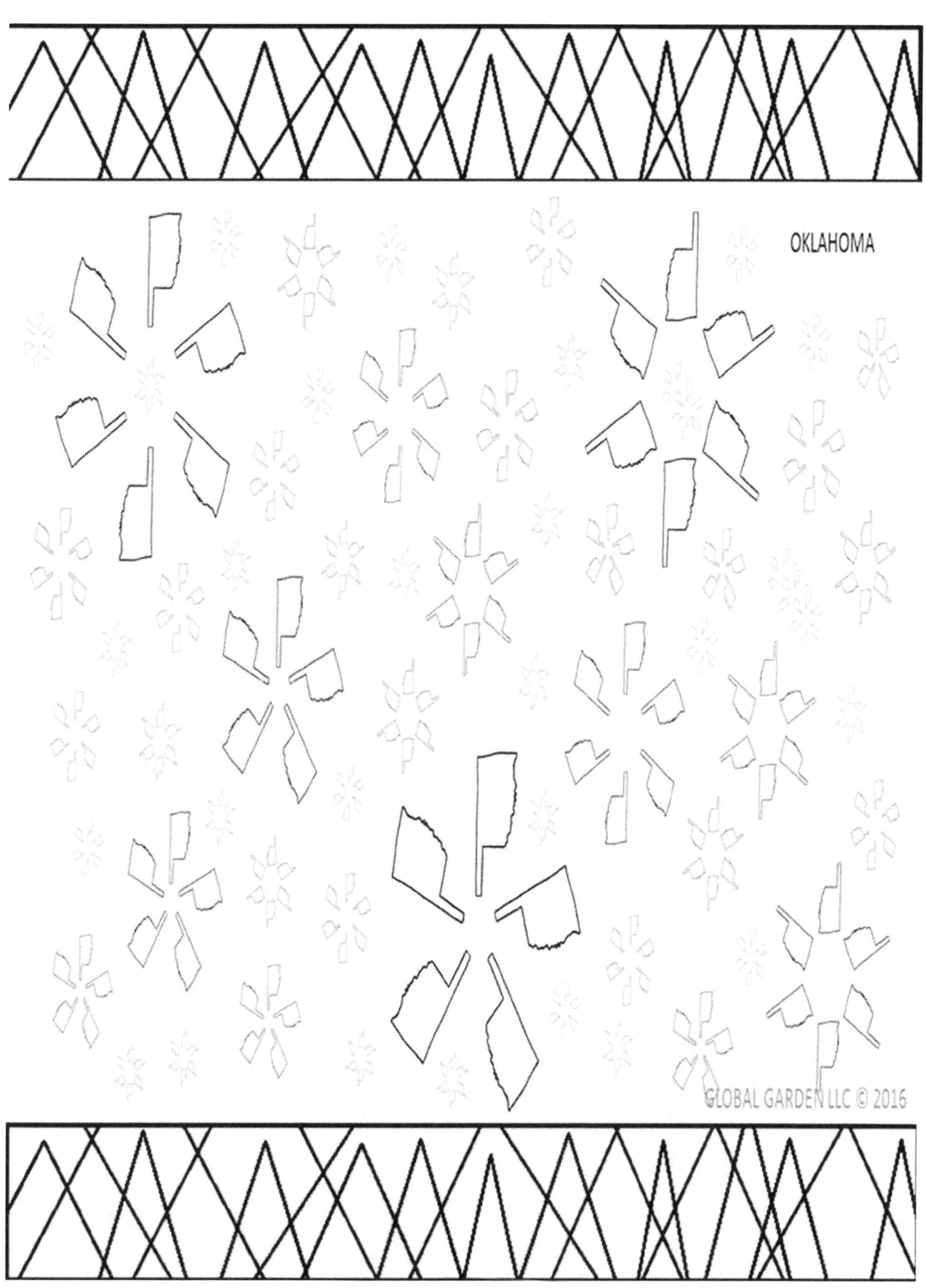

OKLAHOMA

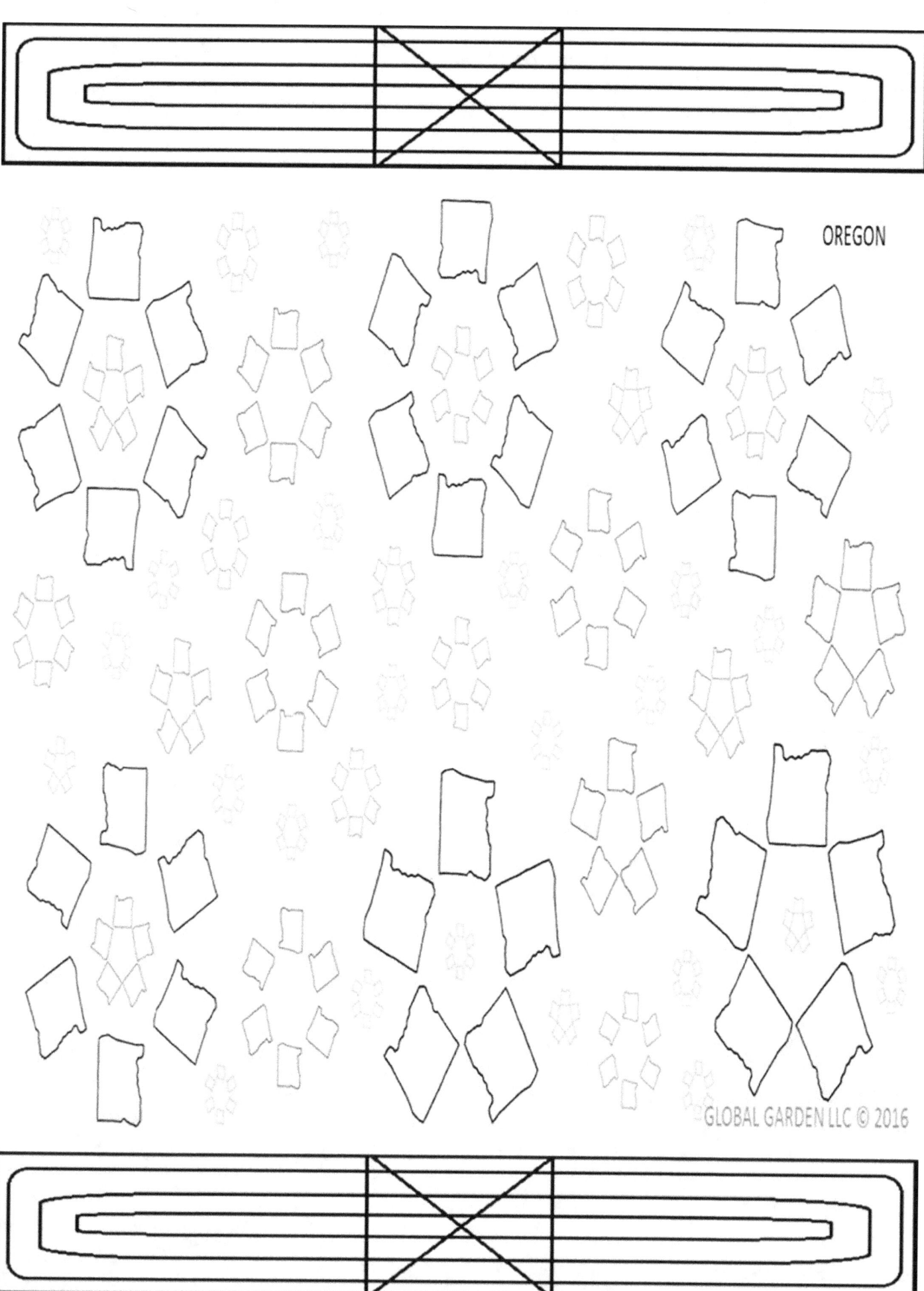

OREGON

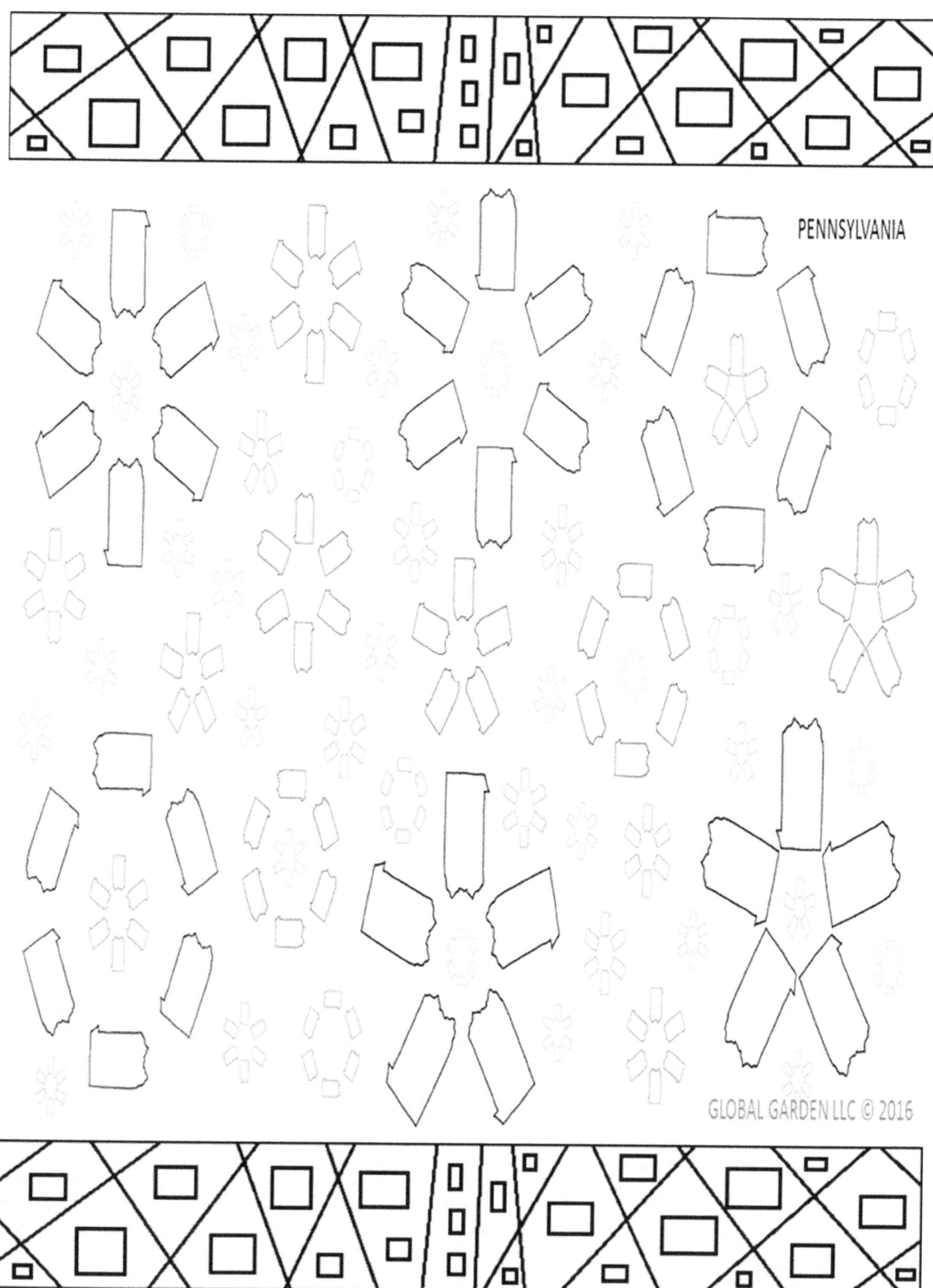

PENNSYLVANIA

GLOBAL GARDEN LLC © 2016

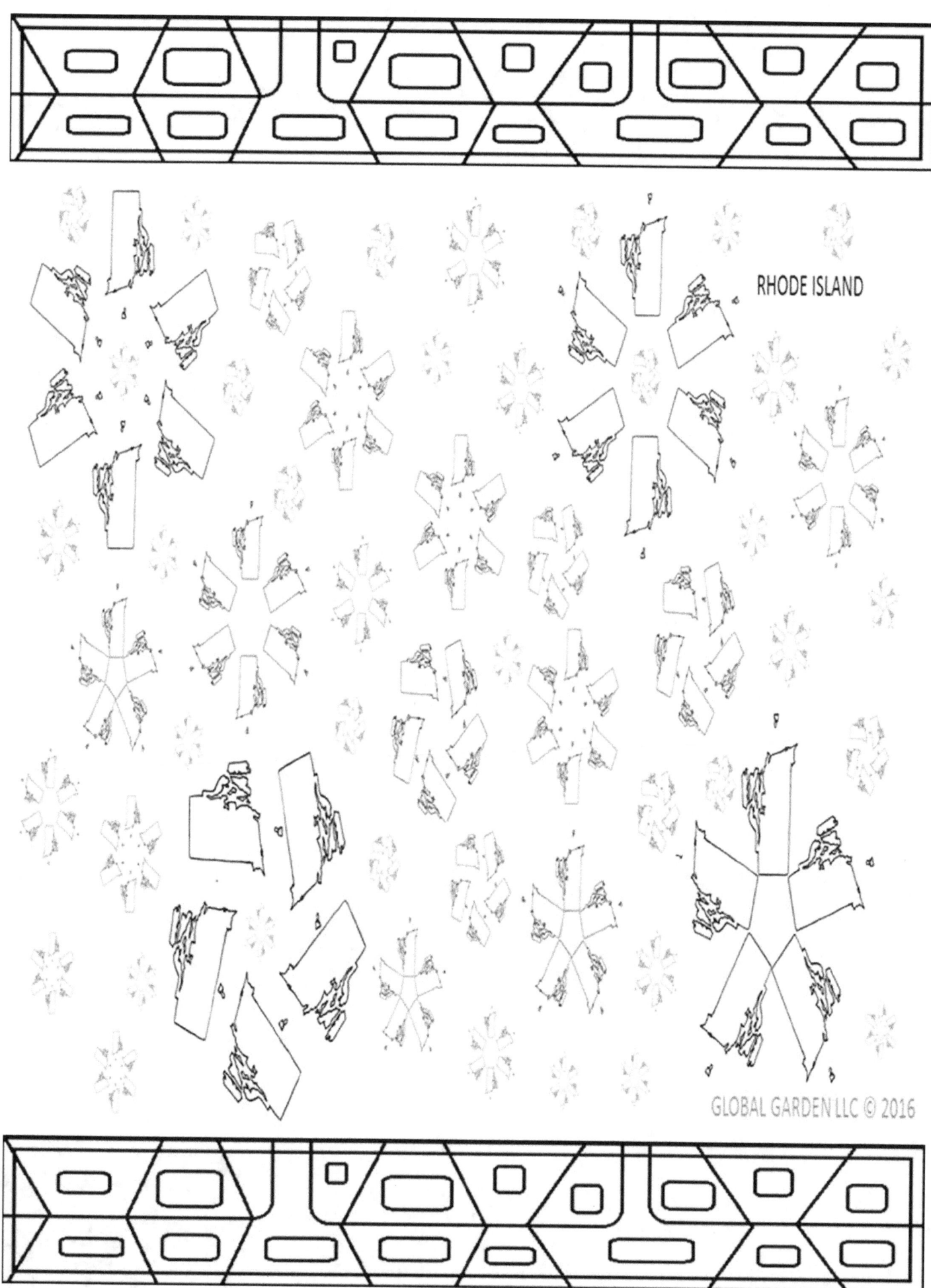

RHODE ISLAND

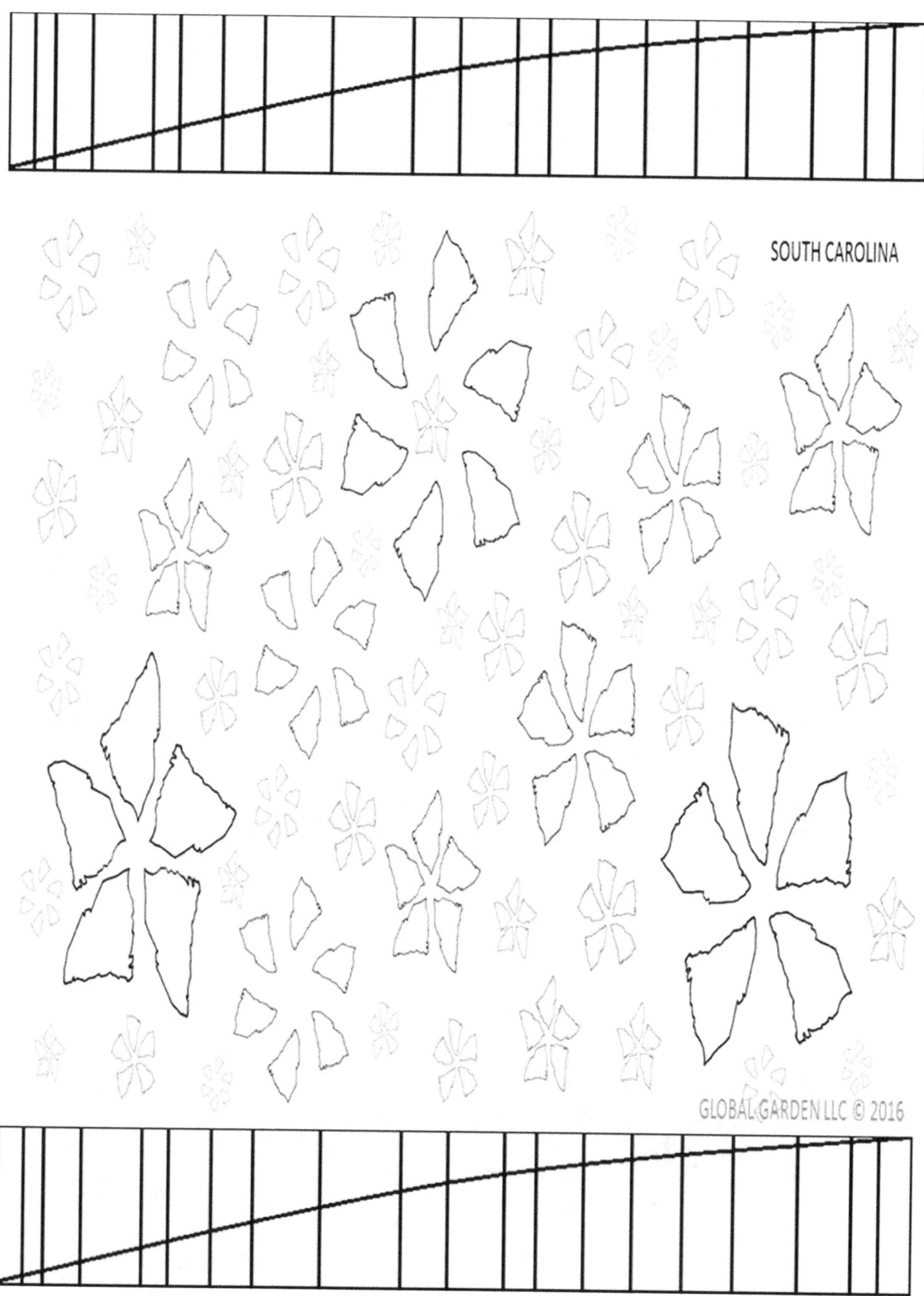

SOUTH CAROLINA

GLOBAL GARDEN LLC © 2016

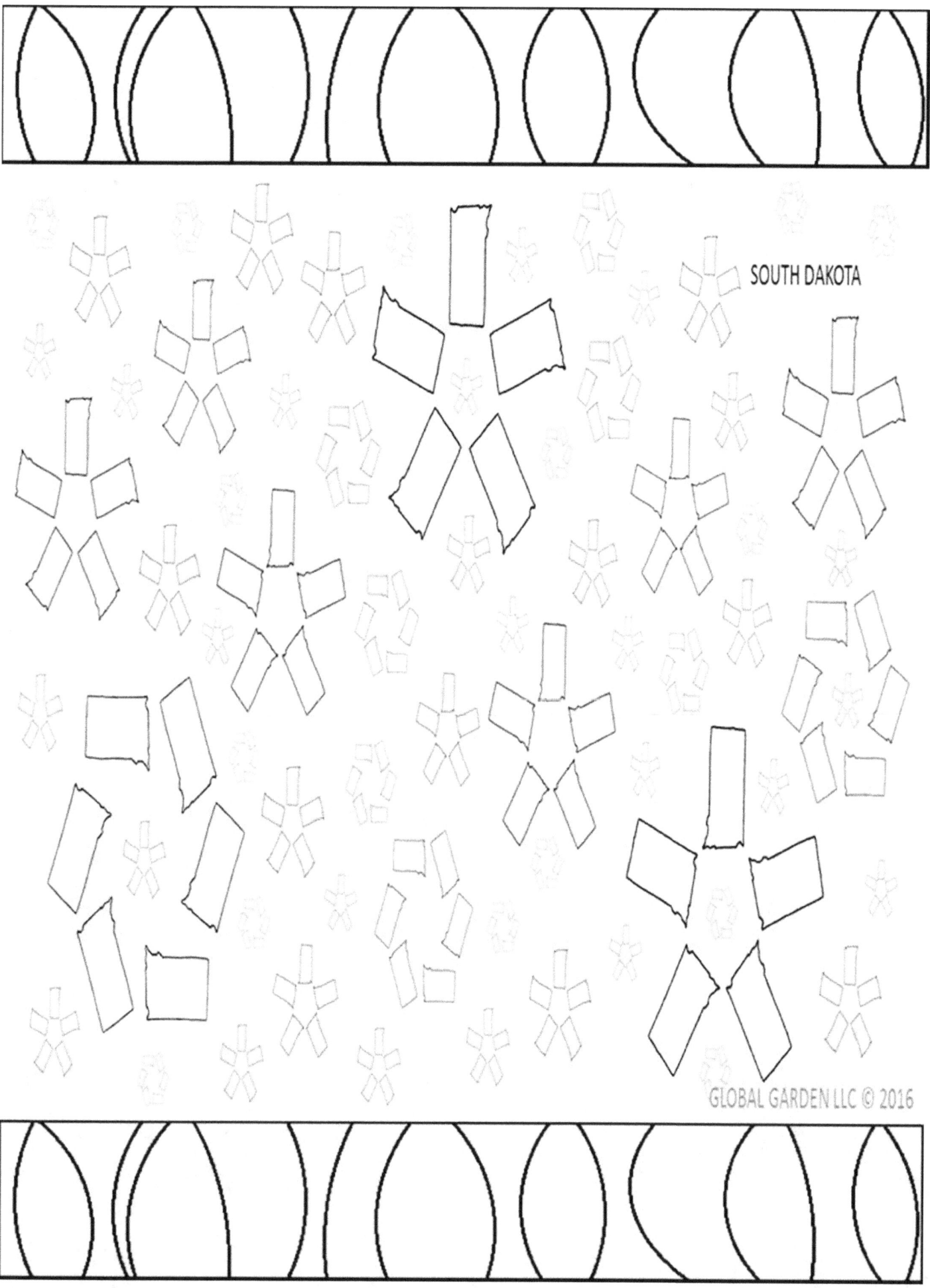

SOUTH DAKOTA

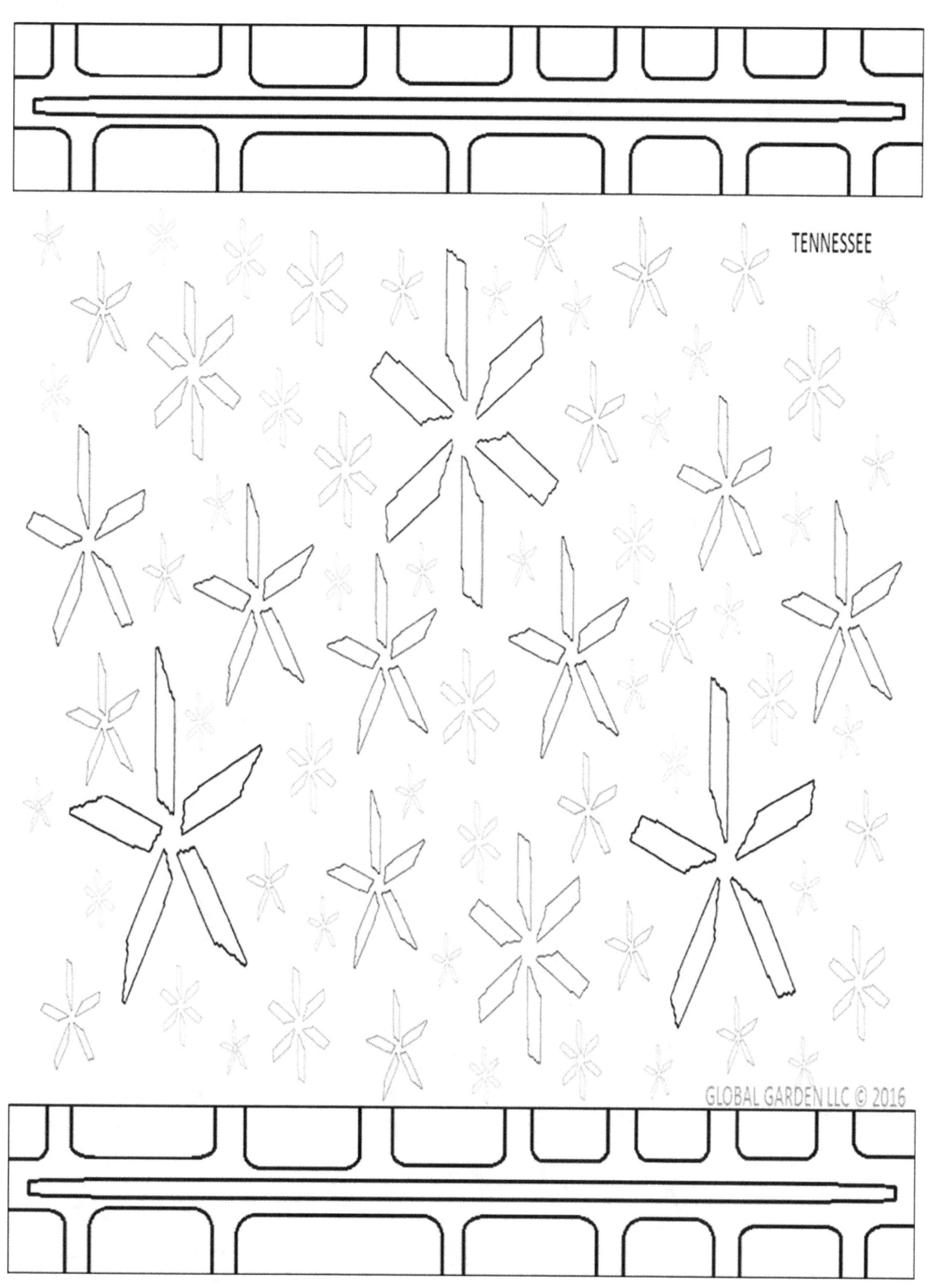

TENNESSEE

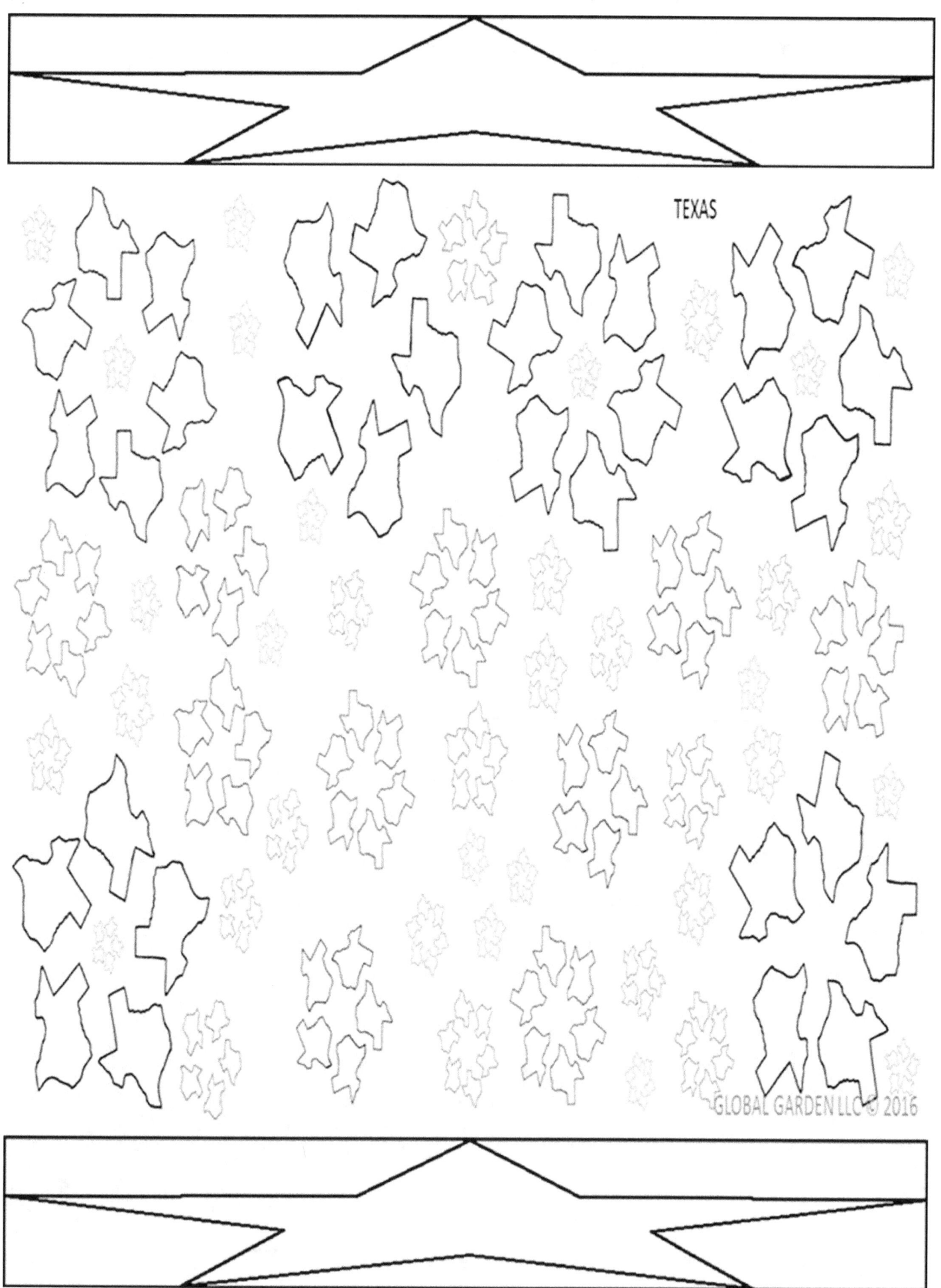

TEXAS

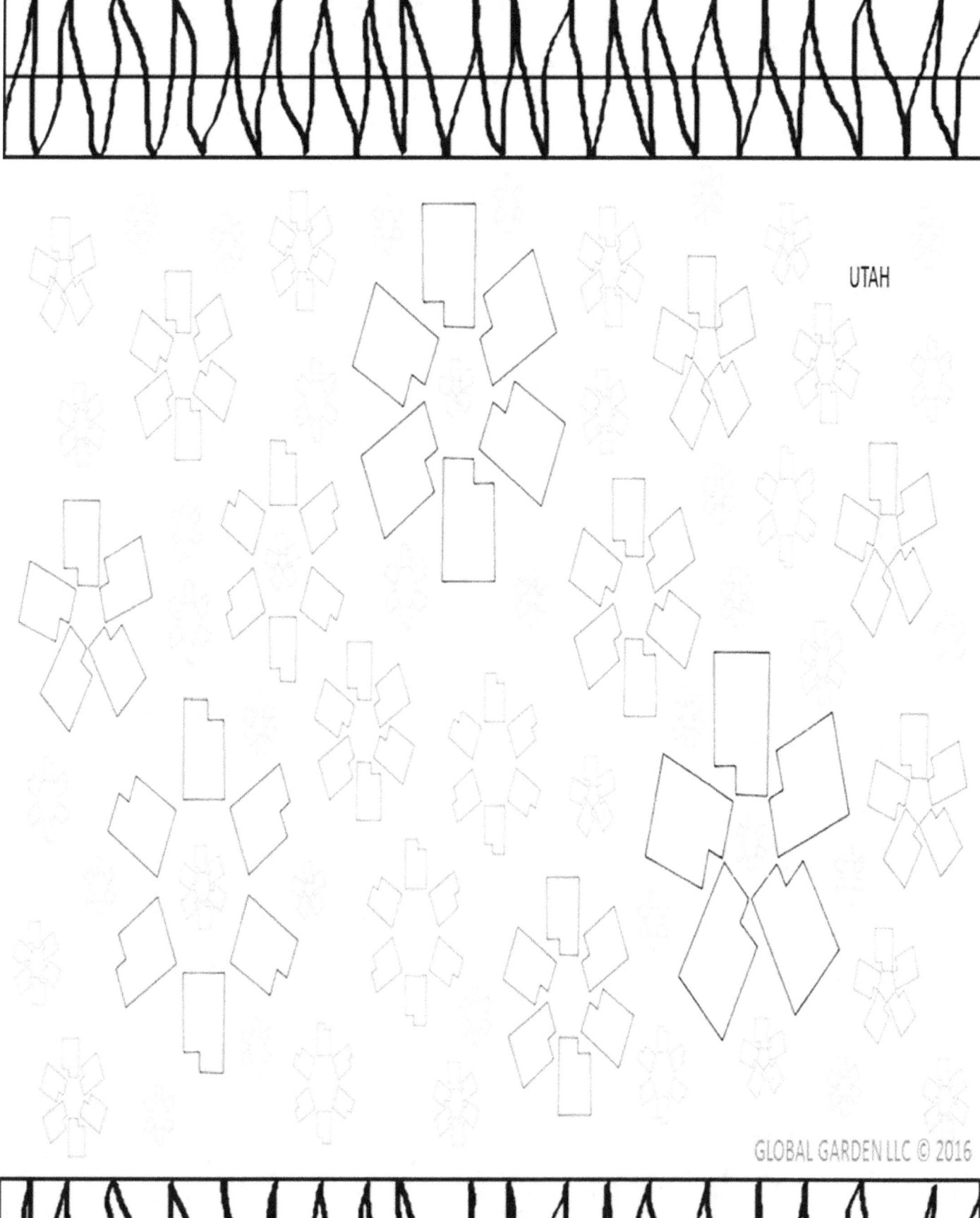

UTAH

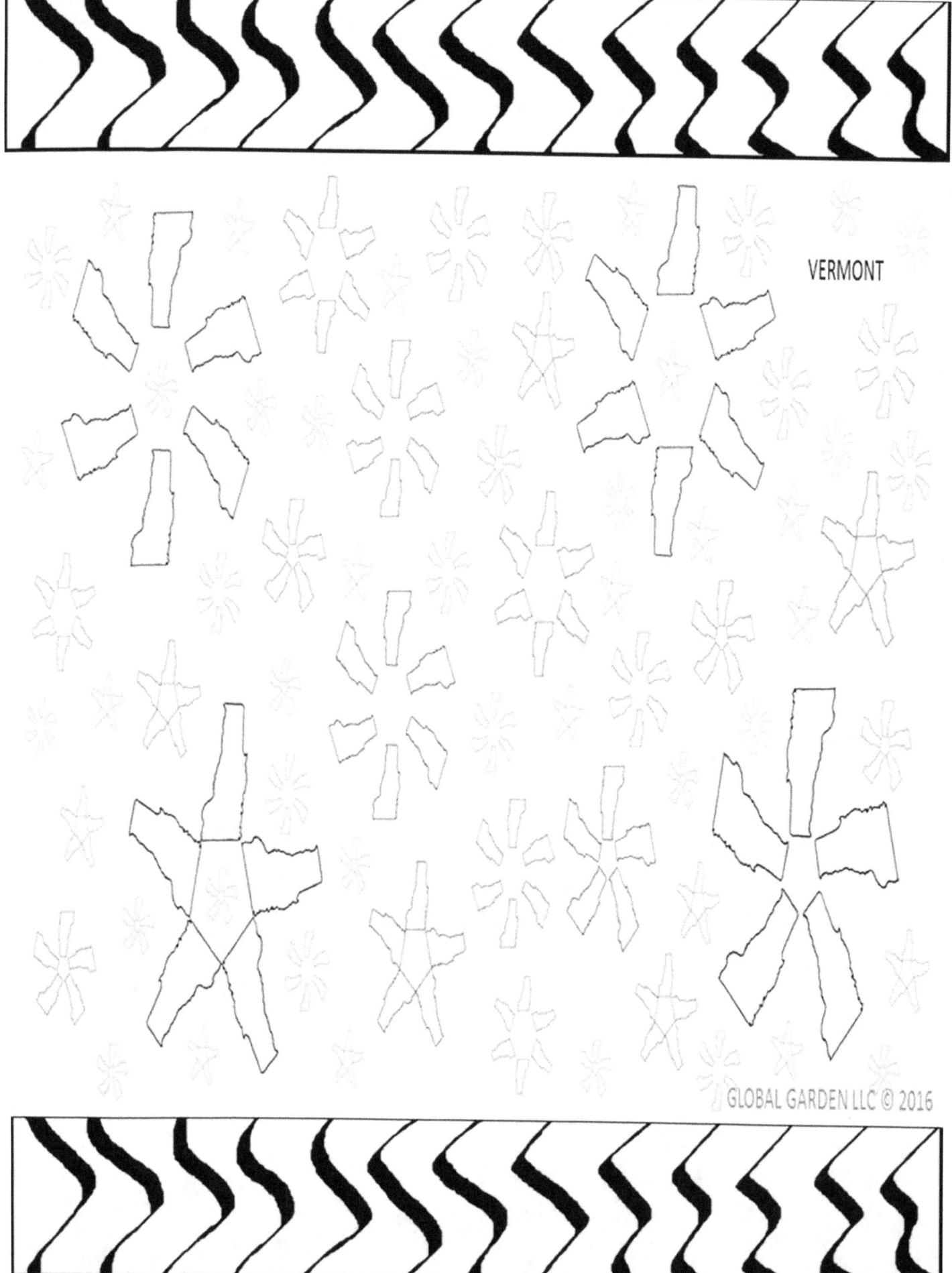

VERMONT

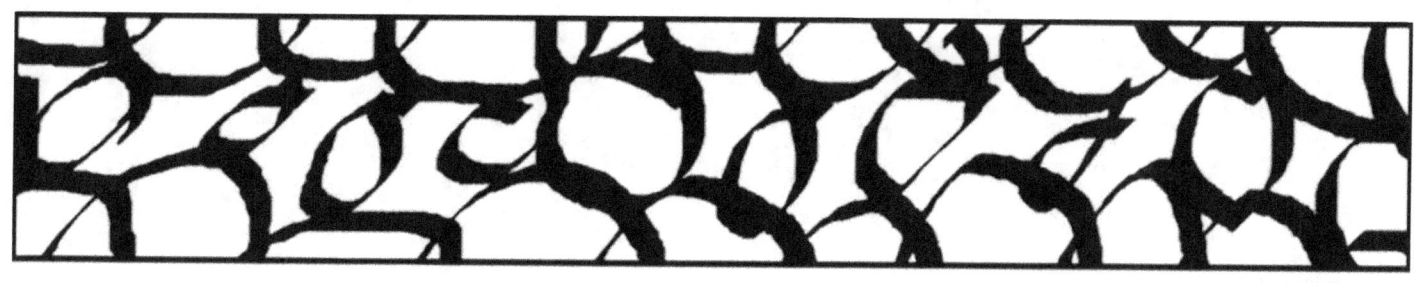

VIRGINIA

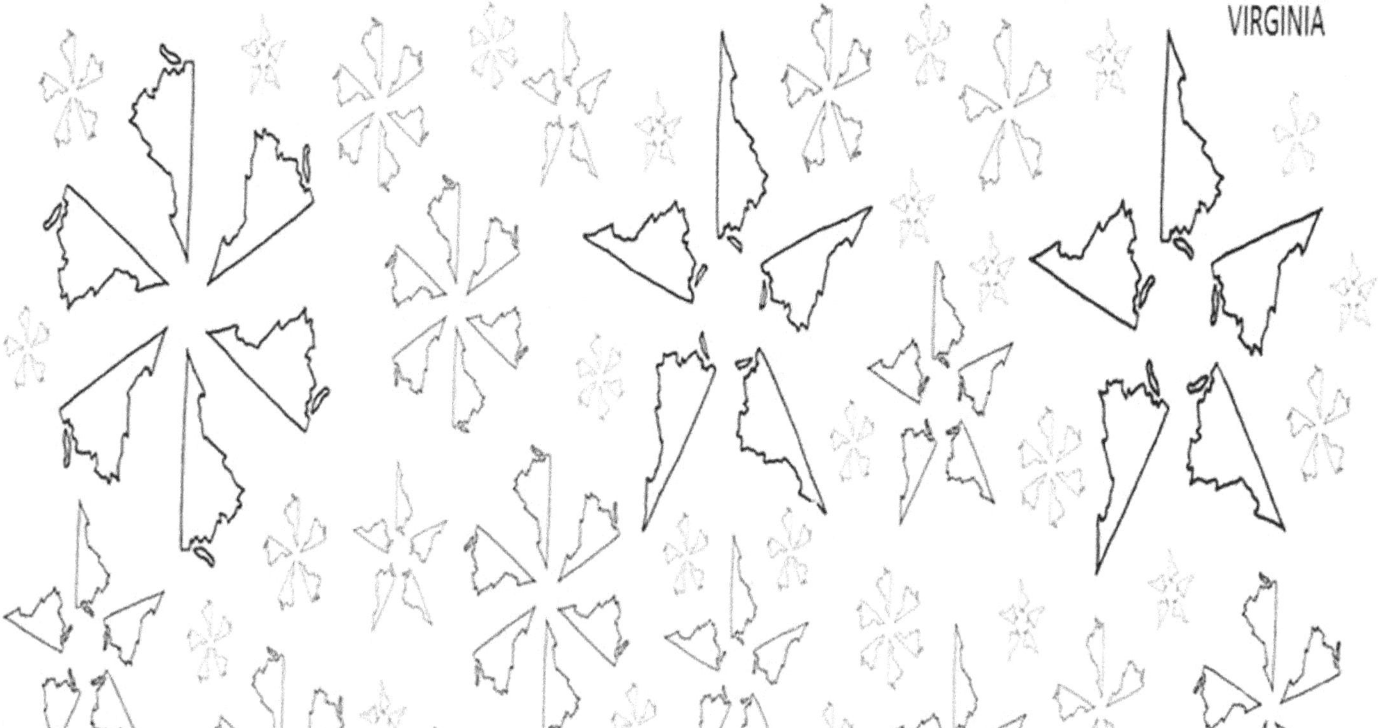

GLOBAL GARDEN LLC © 2016

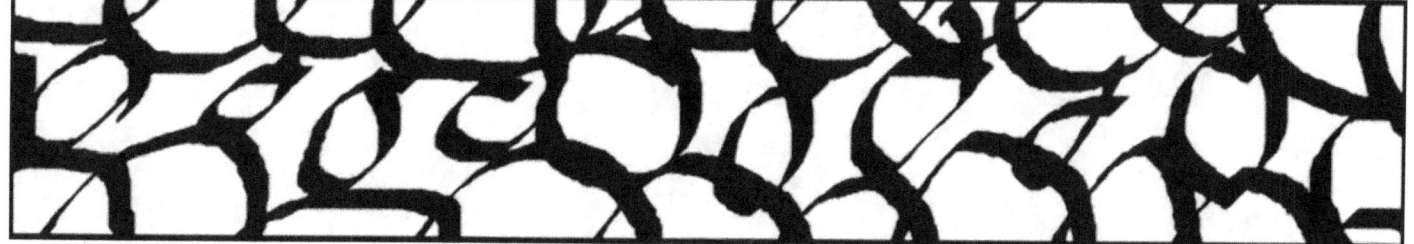

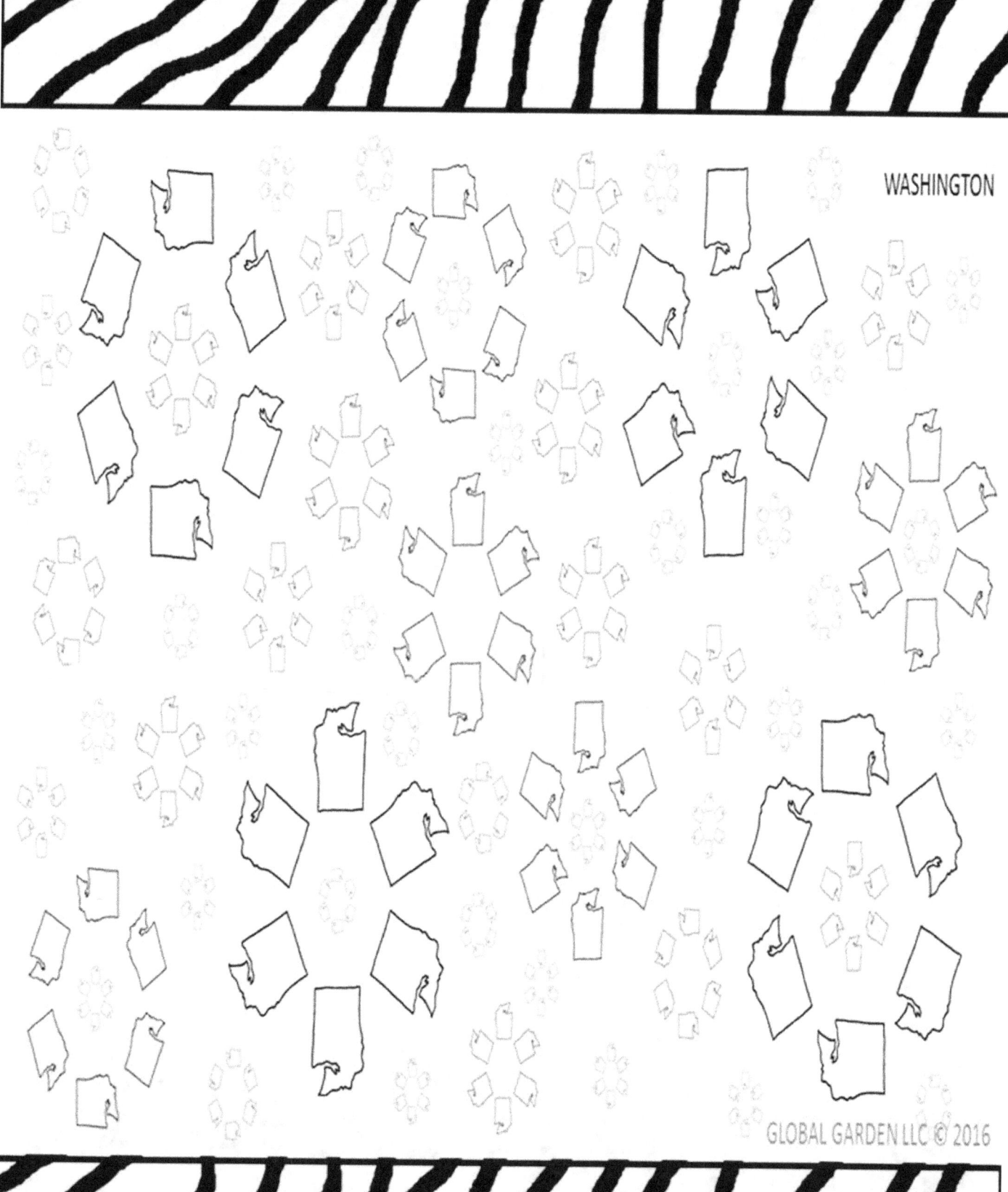

WASHINGTON

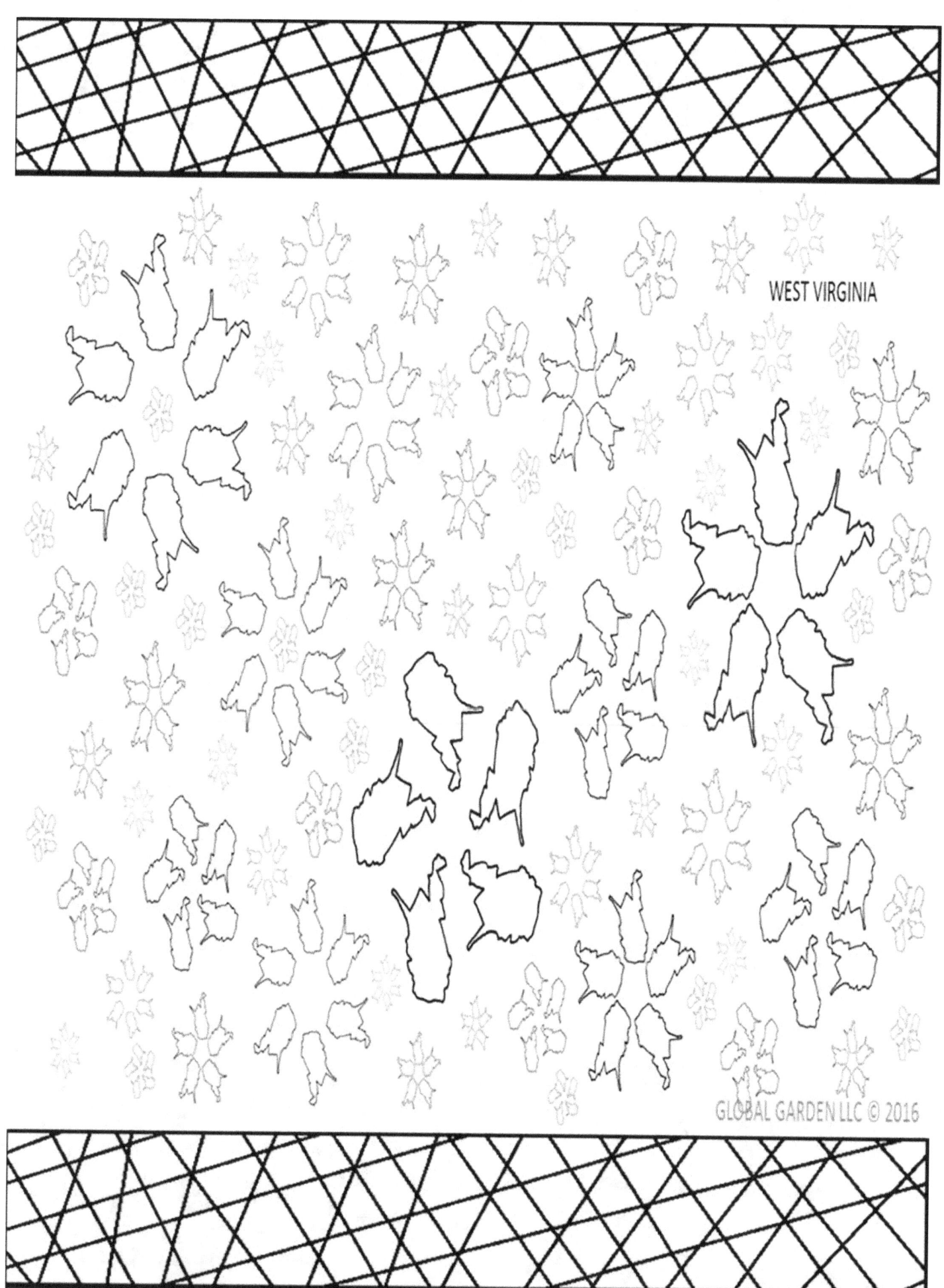

WEST VIRGINIA

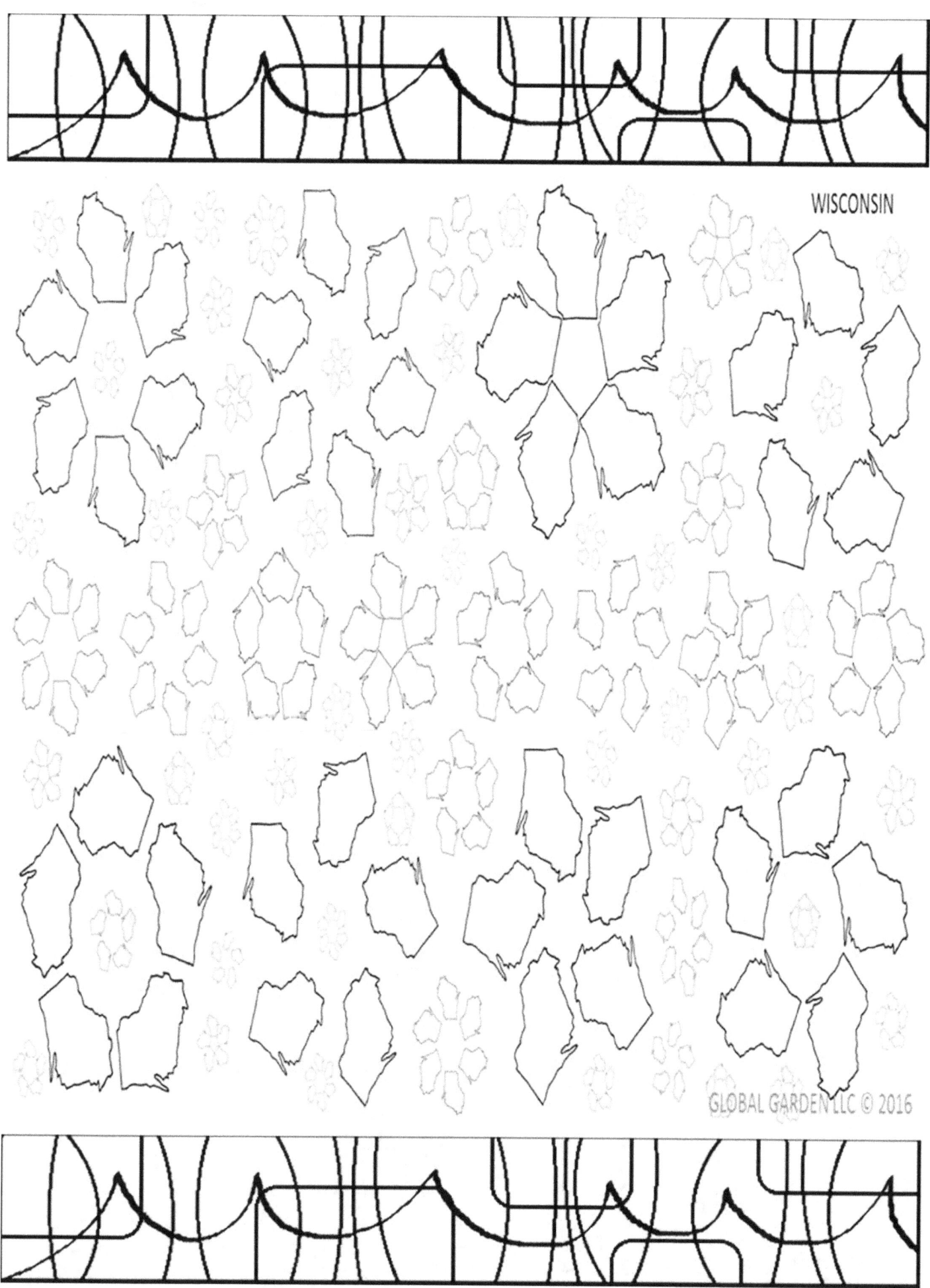

WISCONSIN

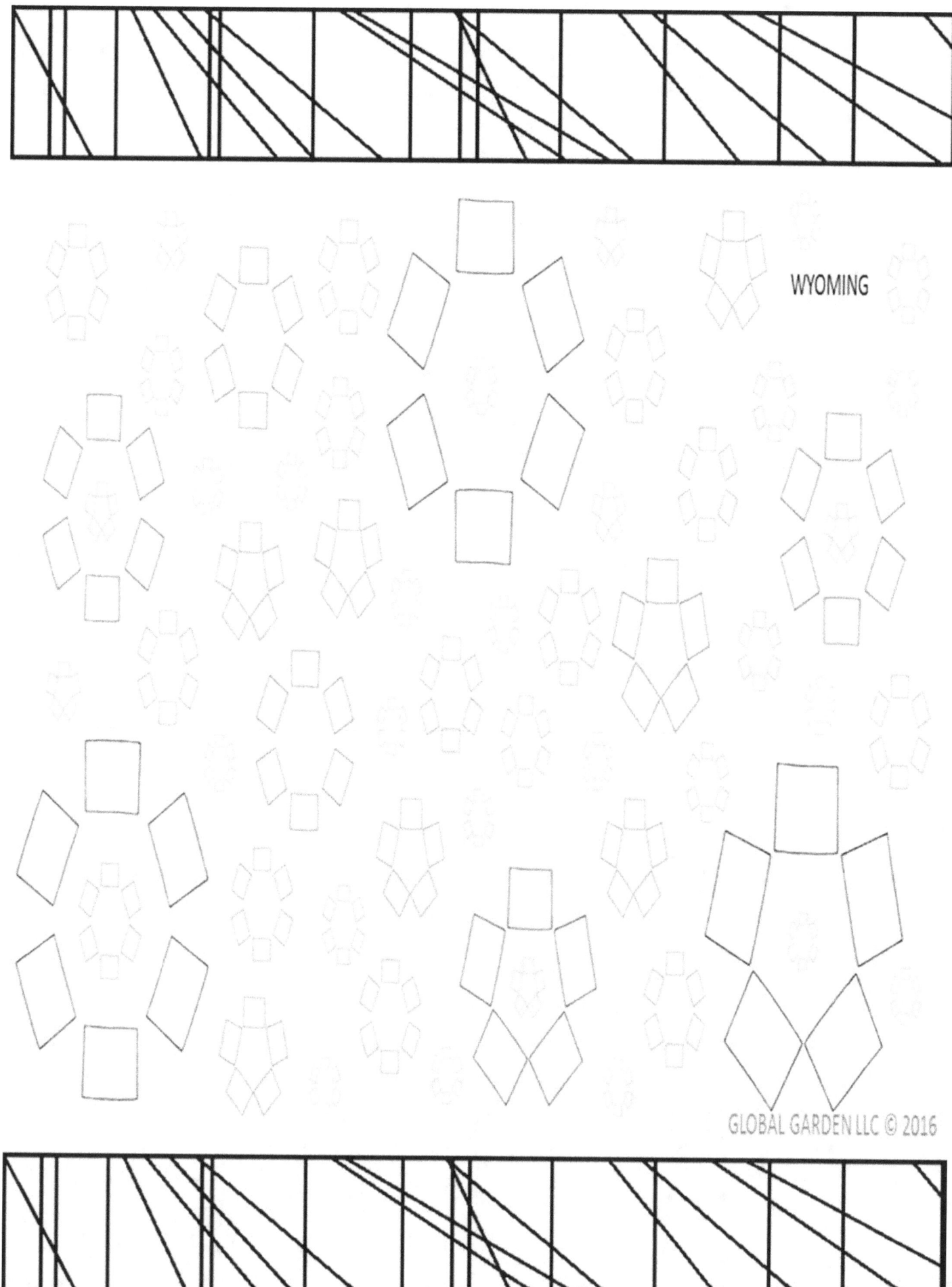

WYOMING